IMAGES
of America

VICTORIAN
FALLS CHURCH

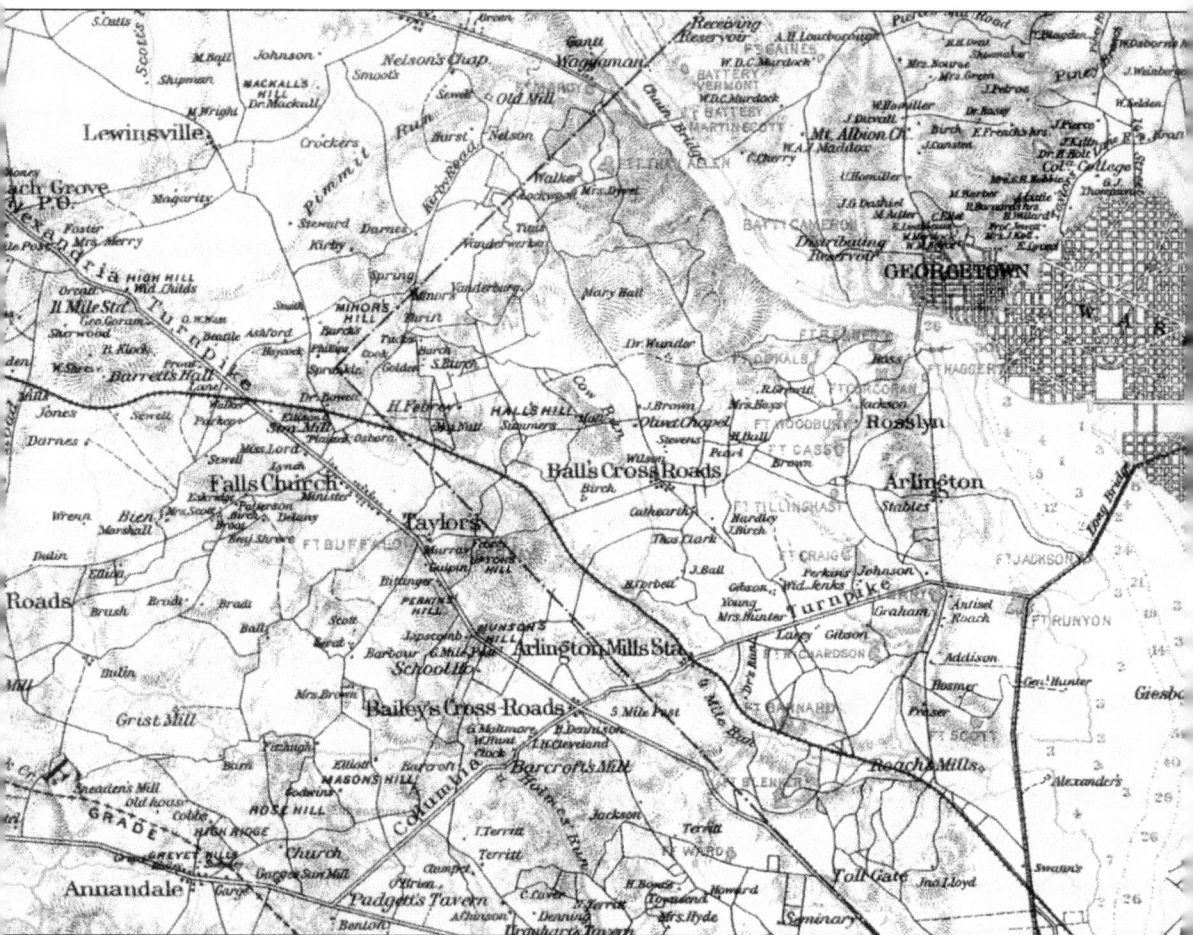

This Civil War–era map, drawn by the federal government, shows Falls Church's close proximity to Washington, D.C. According to the 1860 census, there were 31 families within the current Falls Church city area. Of those, 22 household heads were from northern states. During the Civil War, threatened violence caused many families to leave, and by the war's end, the village population had decreased by almost two-thirds.

ON THE COVER: Every Independence Day, the Falls Church Village Improvement Society sponsored a full-day celebration featuring bands, patriotic exercises and speeches, sporting events, and a barbeque. In this *c.* 1897 photograph, a group of family and friends have found the lawn of the Eagle House Hotel the perfect spot to celebrate the Fourth of July and to have their picture taken. (Courtesy Falls Church Public Library.)

IMAGES
of America

VICTORIAN
FALLS CHURCH

The Victorian Society at Falls Church

ARCADIA
PUBLISHING

Published by Arcadia Publishing
Charleston, South Carolina

Library of Congress Catalog Card Number: 2007921377

For all general information contact Arcadia Publishing at:
Telephone 843-853-2070
Fax 843-853-0044
E-mail sales@arcadiapublishing.com
For customer service and orders:
Toll-Free 1-888-313-2665

Visit us on the Internet at www.arcadiapublishing.com

Mary, Margaret, and Jeanne Riley show off their splendid bustle dresses in this late-1880s photograph that was most likely taken in the yard of their Cherry Hill Farmhouse. (Courtesy Cherry Hill.)

CONTENTS

Acknowledgments   6

Introduction   7

1.   A Village is Born: 1837–1860   9

2.   Division and War: 1861–1865   17

3.   Recovery Spurs Growth: 1866–1879   35

4.   The Town Flourishes: 1880–1889   51

5.   Trolleys and Troops: 1890–1900   65

6.   An Era Ends: 1901–1915   101

Bibliography   127

ACKNOWLEDGMENTS

The Victorian Society at Falls Church (VSFC) is very much indebted to the dedicated librarians and reference staff at the Falls Church Mary Riley Styles Public Library who spent many hours assisting with this effort: Chung Ahn, Brenda Crowley, Janet Daeger-Walden, Lorna Kundert, Marta Lamas, Mary McMahon, Jo Murphy, Shirley Tildon, Lynn Stewart, and Marshall Webster. Unless otherwise noted, all of the images in this book are from the library's Virginia Room collection. Thanks, too, to all those Falls Church residents who over the years donated photographs and historical documentation to the library. Without their donations, this book could not have been written.

Several local families also assisted by providing photographs and family history information. We very much appreciate Catherine Speakman and Ed Henderson for sharing their photographs and Nikki Graves for reviewing photograph narratives relating to the African American community. Thanks also to Diane Morse, curator of Cherry Hill Farmhouse, for providing us with the photograph of the Riley sisters.

The VSFC is extremely fortunate to have a number of authors, historians, and people extremely knowledgeable about Falls Church as members. The contributions of Ron Anzalone, Shirley Camp, Kim Holien, Ross Netherton, Maurice Terman, and Keith Thurston in the writing of the book introduction and the chapter introductions and in the review of the photograph descriptions were a tremendous asset in the development of this book. Thanks also to Terry Hooper and Midge Wang for their help in the photograph selection and editing of the textual materials. Lastly, a special thank you to Linda Lau; she provided the principle motivation and effort that made this book possible.

INTRODUCTION

Falls Church, like so many Colonial Virginia settlements, began as large land grant farms scattered along tobacco rolling roads and anchored by an 18th-century Anglican church and several taverns. Its growth during the Victorian era, roughly parallel to the reign of Queen Victoria in Great Britain (1837–1901) and continuing well into the first quarter of the 20th century, was unremarkable and even typical in many ways. However, its particular history was strongly influenced by its location on the periphery of the national capital of Washington, D.C., by an influx of northern emigrants to the Commonwealth of Virginia in the 1840s and 1850s, by its local witness and participation in the national trauma of the Civil War, and by the interest of its citizens in rebuilding and improving the town after the Civil War.

Originally populated by native people and first explored by English colonists in the years after the 1607 Jamestown settlement, the first Colonial settlement in the area took place in the late 17th and early 18th centuries. By 1734, a frame church had been constructed. In 1769, a brick structure, which still stands as The Falls Church, replaced the deteriorating frame building.

By 1800, the original large landholdings were broken up by multiple heirs and partial sales of property, creating new farms that were generally smaller than before. As much of the soil was exhausted from earlier tobacco harvests, new crops were diversified and included corn, wheat, potatoes, and fruit. Most farmers still owned slaves, and blacks formed a high percentage of the local population. During the next few decades, a continuing agricultural and economic depression caused many farmers to leave the region, particularly freed blacks who had great difficulty earning livelihoods.

The establishment of the federal government in Washington, D.C., figured prominently in Falls Church's growth and development. The increase in travel and trade in the region required the improvement of transportation systems. Completion of the Middle Turnpike, which ran from Alexandria to Dranesville (now Route 7), in 1839 and railroad construction in 1859 ensured that the village, really formed in the late 1850s by numerous small acreage sales near the church, would continue to prosper and grow. That growth would be interrupted during the Civil War years, but after the war, Falls Church soon recovered and resumed its steady improvement throughout the Victorian era. By 1900, it was the largest town in Fairfax County.

While Falls Church was a small provincial community and maintained its village traditions for many years, it was not cut off from the greater world. Many of the residents had come from the northern states or from elsewhere. Some had served in the military and participated in various wars, especially the Civil War. A number of residents worked as government employees in Washington or had business connections to other parts of the country. One resident of the 1850s and 1860s, Star Tavern owner Walter H. Erwin, had participated in the Gold Rush in California. Events and technological advances that affected Victorian America and the rest of the world during these years also affected Falls Church. And although the Victorian era officially ended in 1901 with the death of Queen Victoria, for many the values and traditions of the Victorian era continued through the Edwardian era right up to World War I. Therefore, the story outlined in this book does not end in 1901 with the queen's death but continues through 1915.

Located "on the road to the falls" of the Potomac River in Northern Virginia, 6 miles from Washington, D.C., modern Falls Church is bounded by Arlington County to the northeast and Fairfax County to the north, west, and south. The northeast boundary of modern Falls Church was originally formed by the southwest boundary line for the federal city, laid out in 1791 and delineated by milestone boundary markers. Until 1948, when Falls Church became an independent city and took control of its own schools and municipal services, it was part of Fairfax County.

Today Falls Church retains over 100 structures and sites that date before 1915, the majority of which are locally certified historic structures. Six historic properties, three of which are Victorian-era homes, are listed in the National Register of Historic Places. These include The Falls Church (1769); the 1791 Federal District Boundary Markers, SW 9 (also a National Historic Landmark) and West Cornerstone; Mount Hope (c. 1830 with 1870 addition); the Birch House (c. 1840); and Cherry Hill Farmhouse and Barn (c. 1845). Unfortunately, no commercial structures survive from the period.

Falls Church's Victorian legacy lives on in homes scattered among quiet residential streets or in the public events sponsored by the city (through the Falls Church Historical Commission) and local organizations like the Village Preservation and Improvement Society, the Friends of Cherry Hill, the Tinner Hill Heritage Foundation, and the Victorian Society at Falls Church. In 2007, the Victorian Society at Falls Church published a walking map of Victorian Falls Church, highlighting the remaining Victorian-era buildings and their architectural style as well as the Victorian history of Falls Church.

Perhaps the best description of Victorian Falls Church was made by Elizabeth M. Styles, the granddaughter of Joseph M. Riley, owner of Cherry Hill Farm and a major proponent for the town's charter in 1875. Elizabeth was born in 1893 and spent many childhood summers at Cherry Hill. In 1908, she and her parents moved from Philadelphia to Falls Church where she lived until her death in 1981. Interviewed in 1971 by historian Tony Wrenn, Elizabeth reminisced: "Falls Church to me was a delightful little village. It was a village—an honest to goodness village. You had brick sidewalks which the Village Improvement Society built, and then you had oil lamps on the street. Nearly everybody in town, as far as I can remember now, had from half acre to an acre of ground. Everybody knew everybody, and there was a delightful atmosphere about this town."

One

A VILLAGE IS BORN
1837–1860

The years 1837 through 1860 brought an influx of immigrants from northern states to the area around The Falls Church. Land prices were a fraction of those in New York and New England, and Northern Virginia had a longer growing season than those northern areas. Small tracts of 10 to 75 acres were bought from the few Virginia families who owned then-nonproductive plantations for which slave labor had become unprofitable. The majority of these small-scale farmers labored for themselves with the aid of their families. They used more advanced farming techniques that included fertilizing the ground and using plows with shears to turn over virgin soil. Yields surged to unimaginable heights, and that, as well as extravagant advertisements by enterprising realtors, kept buyers coming.

The Middle Turnpike (now Route 7), an improved road to market in Alexandria, eliminated the meanders in the rolling road but also charged tolls. With increased demand for fresh fruits, vegetables, eggs, meat, and firewood, prices steadily increased to the benefit of the seller. In 1849, there were a sufficient number of citizens for Falls Church to be awarded a post office, and the community was officially considered a village. There was a small, free black community a short distance from The Falls Church inhabited by members who had purchased or been given their freedom.

A schoolhouse built of logs occupied a lot in the center of the village. The school in the Columbia Baptist Church had more advanced classes and was, for a time, run by a woman. Beside schoolteachers, the occupations in the village included a blacksmith, carpenter, shoemaker, cooper, wagon maker, merchant, storekeeper, physician, milliner, and an insurance agent. Most men classified themselves as farmers for the term indicated they were landowners.

The land right-of-way for the Alexandria, Loudoun and Hampshire Railroad (named for three counties it was to traverse) was bought from Falls Church farmers in 1855. By 1860, the line had opened for operation from Alexandria to Leesburg.

The future was bright with expectations for the continued growth of the village of Falls Church.

Big Chimneys, shown here in a modern drawing, is believed to have been the first permanent structure built in Falls Church. The large log house was named for its two huge chimneys; one chimney had a date stone inscribed 1699, which is the date traditionally used for the community's founding. It was torn down between 1908 and 1914.

In 1790, after much debate, Congress chose a Potomac River site for the new national capital. Boundary stones were placed to mark the boundary of the 10-mile-square district that would become the new federal city. In 1846, Congress returned the portion of the district that was west of the Potomac River to Virginia. Two of the original markers are on the Falls Church boundary line.

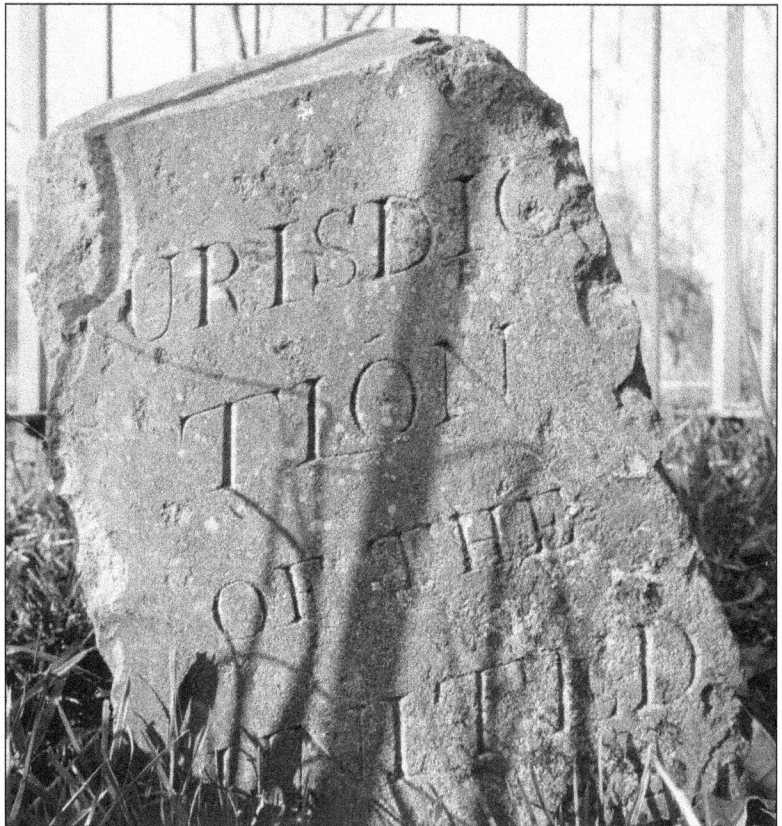

The Middle Turnpike (also called the Leesburg and Alexandria Turnpike), now Route 7, was completed in 1839 and was so named because it was between the Georgetown and Little River Turnpikes. The tollgate site, pictured in a sketch drawn in 1874, collected tolls until 1872 when Fairfax County bought the turnpike for $300.

The frame part of Mount Hope shown in a 20th-century photograph may have been built in 1830. The house and farm were purchased in 1842 by Amzi Coe, an immigrant from New York, who named it Mount Hope. It was the earliest known stop on the Falls Church mail route and, until about 1857, served as the first meeting place for the Presbyterians in Falls Church.

Cherry Hill Farmhouse was built c. 1845 on property once part of the Trammell grant of 1729. The timber-frame barn was built about 1856; other buildings included a corn crib, well house, and necessary (outhouse). It has a long history, especially related to the Joseph Riley family. Now a historic site open to the public, the house is furnished much as it would have been in the 1850s.

Built c. 1845 "for religious and other services," Groot Hall was used not only for Presbyterian church services but also served as home for the Groot Hall Academy, which held its classes upstairs. In this c. 1908 photograph, Groot Hall can be seen behind the church group. The hall was torn down in 1925.

The earliest portion of this large, clapboard house was built during the 1840s. In 1852, Joseph E. Birch, a farmer and blacksmith, purchased it and 12 acres for $483.75. The family made major additions to the house in the 1870s, and in style, the house looks more Victorian than its antebellum date would indicate. The Birch family lived in the house until 1968.

Joseph E. Birch, shown with his first wife, Delphina Orton Birch, was born in Alexandria County but moved to Falls Church in 1841 and would live there until his death in 1892. A community leader, he was a member of the first town council and was instrumental in founding the Jefferson Institute. This photograph was taken before Delphina's death from consumption in 1853 at the age of 22.

George B. Ives bought this Italianate-style house for $400. Built in 1854, Ives lived in the house from 1860 until his death in 1914. He was known for his skill at carpentry; during the 1850s, he possibly worked on nearly every house in Falls Church as well as Groot Hall and Columbia Baptist Church. He was named postmaster in 1862 and was mayor of the town in 1878.

The Andrew Ellison family built this brick home, called "Ivy Knoll," around 1855. In 1883, it was purchased by Judge Ambrose Rowell and his wife who were great gardeners; they added the glass conservatory that is pictured. The grounds were known for their blooming flowers and beautiful shade trees, especially elm and maple. In 1979, the house was greatly modified to be part of an office complex.

Fairmont, pictured in the 1880s, was built 30 years earlier by John E. Febrey, a prominent Falls Church citizen and a well-to-do farmer and realtor. At some point, the house was totally rebuilt or remodeled to a more impressive mansion. The house is still standing in 2007 at the corner of McKinley Street and Wilson Boulevard.

William Henry Ellison was a carpenter and builder by trade. In 1851, he relocated from Alexandria, Virginia, to Falls Church and in 1852 completed this large farmhouse that was located at the corner of Broad Street and West Street. The Falls Church Library was once housed here. It was torn down in 1955, and a gas station is now on this site.

The advent of a steam engine locomotive in the 1820s made railway service practical, and communities soon realized its potential for moving both freight and passengers. In 1847, the Virginia General Assembly chartered the Alexandria and Harper's Ferry Railroad Company to establish a line between those two points, which would also run through Falls Church. In 1854, the company's name was changed to the Alexandria, Loudoun and Hampshire Railroad Company, and in 1855, work actually began on the line. Sections of the line were operational in 1858, and by the spring of 1861, the full line was open. In 1860, the 35-minute ride from Falls Church to Alexandria cost 50¢. The top photograph is the East Falls Church train station; the bottom photograph is the West Falls Church station and train tracks.

Two

DIVISION AND WAR
1861–1865

During the tragedy that was to befall America from 1861 to 1865, the peaceful village of Falls Church played a role that mirrored that of America. It was a divided village in a divided state in a divided nation. Its citizens came from both the North and the South, and were both black and white.

When the storm clouds of war broke forth over America in April 1861, few could foresee the harbinger of events to come to Falls Church. Here families were divided, friends separated, and the war that many supposed would last only as long as a summer storm ravaged the young American nation for four years.

After their July 21 victory at Bull Run, the Confederate forces occupied Falls Church for about two months, but then the Union troops returned to the area for the rest of the war and constructed several forts on the hills southeast of the village. Though no major battles were to be fought within its boundaries, there occurred numerous skirmishes (firefights in modern military parlance). Soldiers were taken prisoner, wounded, killed, and buried here just as they were at Gettysburg. Though enemies, they were still Americans and often left notes and calling cards for each other. Civilians, too, suffered. Their homes, farms, and churches were looted, damaged, and in some cases totally destroyed by troops from both sides.

Spies, male and female, military and civilian, black and white, abounded as Falls Church became a floating no-man's-land between the armies of the Blue and the Gray. Forts were built, signal flags waved their wigwag, and makeshift hospitals nurtured the sick and wounded. Here Prof. Thaddeus Lowe launched his famous reconnaissance balloons in and about the village of Falls Church. The famous "Gray Ghost" of the Confederacy, Col. John Singleton Mosby, led many a raid in and around Falls Church. These raids created consternation but had little effect on the final outcome.

At the war's end, the remaining villagers, joined by new arrivals, began the long road to recovery.

"The Ordinance of Secession":
Poll taken at Falls Church, Fairfax County Virginia, Va, on Thursday the 23rd day of May 1861, upon the Ratification or Rejection of "An Ordinance to repeal the ratification of the Constitution of the United States of America, by the State of Virginia, and to resume all the rights and powers granted under said Constitution, adopted in Convention at the City of Richmond on the 17th day of April 1861 —

For Ratification		For rejection	
W F Dulany	1	D H Dulany	1
J E Birch	2	H W Throckmorton	2
Craven Ashford	3	Benjamin Block	3
C. H. Newton	4	Josiah Galpin	4
Charles C. Ashford	5	W Clover	5
F. H. C. Terrett	6	W H Ellison	6
H. H. Shreve	7	John Bartlett	7
A. H. Darne	8	W H Erwin	8
James H. Haycock	9	Seth Osborn	9
Charles Binns	10	Ruben Ives	10
J. M. Fitzhugh	11	George B Ives	11
George Minor	12	J J Groot	12
W H Sewell	13	Silas osborne	13
Richard H. Wheeler	14	James Bennett	14
Saml R Johnston	15	Albert H Ives	15
G. H. Terrett	16	Levi Parker	16
Rich'd J Rockford	17	J M Haycock	17
G. W West	18		
John A Mills	19		
A B Allen	20		
J M Brush	21		

Talk of Virginia's secession from the Union and the pending Civil War caused a large rift in the Falls Church community. Families and friends splintered as those from the South generally favored secession, and those from the North were pro-Union. On April 27, 1861, the Virginia General Assembly voted to secede pending a statewide referendum set for May 23. At that time, there were no secret ballots. Those men who voted in Falls Church went to poll judges (often pro-secessionist) who announced their vote. Their votes were then recorded in the ledger, shown. Because of threats and intimidation, many pro-Union residents chose not to vote or had already left the area. As a Unionist recalled, "When the secession movement commenced, Union men were threatened if they did not leave."

18

For ratification		For rejection	
George P. Kirby	23	Wm. Hatch	18
George M. Mills	24	Andrew Ellison	19
Charles J. Estridge	25	A. J. Sines	20
Lisander Then	26	Andrew Beadle	21
Thomas J. Haycock	27	John Cornwell	22
W. L. Sewall	28	Arther West	23
J. C. Mills	29	Wm. C. Lipscomb	24
Aaron Bratt	30	Nicholas Groosbeck	25
John C. Sewall	31	W. A. Blasedale	26
Darius Prout	32		
William Shreve	33		
W. C. Slade	34		
James J. Robey	35		
Edward W. Crump	36		
W. J. Bailey	37		
Nicholas Lemen	38		
William Linch	39		
E. F. Crump	40		
John Brown	41		
Charles Then	42		
Albert Then	43		
John B. Goram	44		

John W. Lynch, a pro-Unionist had intended to vote but didn't: "I did not vote on ratifying the Ordinance of Secession. I went to the polls for the purpose of voting against the Ordinance . . . and I was told if I did so, I would be regarded as a traitor. Benjamin F. Shreve, one of the judges, told me this. I went away and did not vote. There were five or seven walked away at the same time, and did not vote." The ledger clearly shows exactly how each man voted. In the end, 44 voted to secede and 26 voted against secession. Considering the threats and intimidations that were made to the men and their families, it was a reasonably close vote.

William Henry Lynch and his wife, Elizabeth Ellen Lightfoot Lynch, were ardent secessionists. Not liking it that Union troops were stationed at Falls Church, William used his young son, Nathan, as a spy, sitting the boy on a fence in the village center so he could observe troop movements. William, a well-respected blacksmith, was jailed several times for his Confederate spy activities. In September 1861, Union artillery, under direction from an observer in a balloon, fired on Falls Church, which was then occupied by Confederates. Elizabeth fled with her children to a nearby plantation until the firing ended. Upon her return, she found several household items missing and attributed their disappearance to Union troops. Ellen was obviously not a vindictive woman. When later feeding a hungry Union colonel, she said she was willing to feed any hungry person, "even a Yankee."

Born on the eve of the Civil War in December 1860, Ann Valinda Lynch would spend her first few years in the midst of war, fleeing with her mother as Union troops fired on their home. This charming photograph shows how a typical child of the 1860s would have dressed. In 1881, Ann married Charles E. Mankin, a successful merchant, and lived in Falls Church until her death in 1925.

Built in 1854 this Greek Revival–style house, named "Home Hill," was owned by John Bartlett, a New York native who was a farmer and Treasury Department employee. The house was one of the largest around Falls Church. The Confederates, who did not want to punish Southern sympathizers, chose this house as their command headquarters when they occupied Falls Church from July 22 to September 29, 1861.

The Columbia Baptist Church was completed in 1858 at its original location at 160 E. Broad Street. The membership of about 90 people appears to have included local African Americans. Then minister, Hiram Read, was an ardent abolitionist. He also instituted a high school in the building with a woman as principal. The advent of war had a devastating affect on the congregation; many left the area. During the first two years of war, the church was used as a hospital, which housed the wounded from both factions. School was resumed after the war, and the congregation reorganized in 1879. A petition to the federal government for damage done by Union troops resulted in a payment of $800 for repairs. This photograph, with noted early photographer Mathew Brady in the foreground, was taken c. 1862.

In mid-June 1861, Union
general Daniel Tyler
with troops from several
Connecticut regiments,
established headquarters
at Taylor's Tavern.
The tavern, owned by
William H. Taylor, was
located on a hill at what
is today E. Broad Street
between Roosevelt Street
and Wilson Boulevard.
Mathew Brady took this
photograph, c. 1862.

This June 1861 engraving from *Frank Leslie's Illustrated Newspaper* shows the Connecticut militia
arriving in Falls Church. The unidentified building shown is not Taylor's Tavern, although that
is where the militia camped. The camp at Taylor's Hill would be named Camp Tyler in honor of
Union general Daniel Tyler.

On June 22, 1861, Thaddeus Lowe, a self-described "aeronaut," inflated his balloon at the D.C. gasworks, and soldiers then walked it out to Taylor's Tavern. On June 24–25, Lowe made several tethered ascents, the first aerial reconnaissance in American military history. This engraving from the *New York Illustrated News*, July 1861, shows Lowe going aloft from Falls Church to look at the Confederate forces near the Fairfax Court House.

Star Tavern, as seen in this June 1861 engraving from *Frank Leslie's Illustrated Newspaper*, was built about 1852. Located at what is now the corner of W. Broad and S. Washington Streets, during the war it was occupied by Union forces and at one point was General McClellan's headquarters. The star sign, shown in the engraving, was made of green bottle glass and lighted by a candle.

GENERAL M'CLELLAN OCCUPYING THE CONFEDERATE POSITION AT MUNSON'S HILL.

"Our regiment . . . are encamped in Halls Hill opposite Falls Church, which 4 days ago the Rebels held, but are now driven in all directions. We have taken Munson Hill without firing a single gun. The Rebels are funny ducks. They had erected 2 wooden Cannon painted black to represent that they were fortified," is how a soldier from the 18th Massachusetts described the Union occupation of Munson's Hill.

During the war, Mathew Brady took several photographs of The Falls Church. Originally occupied by Confederates and then by Union forces, the church was used as both a hospital and later as a stable. The church suffered major damage and was nearly gutted; even the floorboards were torn up. The building was saved from demolishment by two local men who appealed to the military commander.

The graffiti shown on the church walls are the names of Union soldiers. An 1865 petition for restitution stated, "We . . . do hereby certify that the tablets, window curtains, blinds, pews and carpeting . . . were removed by Union soldiers." The federal government provided $1,413.50 to restore the church to its prewar condition.

This baptismal font is one of the two surviving items from the prewar church. One day, a Union soldier stopped at Star Tavern and asked the postmistress to send home a package containing "a relic of the old church [George] Washington attended." Realizing that it was from the church, she decided to not send it, hiding the historic stone font until it could be returned.

FALL'S CHURCH, VIRGINIA, THE ADVANCED POST OF OUR ARMY ON THE POTOMAC.

THE REBELS IN VIRGINIA.

WE continue our series of illustrations of THE REBEL ARMY IN VIRGINIA, from sketches by our faithful correspondent. With regard to the illustrations on pages 487 and 491, he writes us: "I send you a sketch of the camp of General Bee's BRIGADE OF THE CONFEDERATE ARMY, at the Fair Grounds near Winchester. It consists of some five regiments of Alabamians and Mississippians, in all about five thousand men. They are camped there at present, awaiting the advance of General Patterson, when I suppose General Johnston will order another retreat. The other sketch is one of a little incident which took place at Harper's Ferry yesterday. Two of the Ninth, Isaac Blakemore and George M'Mullan, went over and climbed the pole in the armory yard and took down the State flag of Virginia, which had been flying there since the place was first occupied by the Confederates. It was brought over to Sandy Hook and divided among their comrades, each one of whom secured a piece to send home as a trophy."

FALL'S CHURCH.

ON this page we illustrate FALL'S CHURCH, FAIRFAX COUNTY, VIRGINIA, from a sketch by our special artist with General M'Dowell's *corps d'armée*. This is the most advanced post of our army in Fairfax County, and has been the scene of several picket skirmishes. Fall's Church was built in 1709, and rebuilt, as an inscription on the wall informs us, by the late "Lord" Fairfax, whose son, the present "Lord" Fairfax, is supposed to be serving in the rebel army. The title of Lord, we may observe, is still given to the representative of the family. The inscription on the old church reads as follows:

"Henry Fairfax, an accomplished gentleman, an upright magistrate, a sincere Christian, died in command of the Fairfax Volunteers at Saltillo, Mexico, 1847. But for his munificence this church might still have been a ruin."

Service was held in the old church two Sundays since—Rev. Dr. Mines, Chaplain of Second Maine Regiment, officiating, and most of the troops in the neighborhood being present.

By the time this engraving was published in *Harper's Weekly* on August 3, 1861, Falls Church was occupied by Confederate troops. This would be short-lived however, as on September 29, the Confederates quietly abandoned Falls Church for positions at Centreville. Union troops quickly reoccupied the village and would fortify some of the hills southeast of the village for the remainder of the war. Armed skirmishes in and around the village were a daily fact of life for those remaining and many residents fled during these times only returning after the war.

Sisters America Virginia Scott and Artemisia Darne Scott of Falls Church were both ardent secessionists. This engraving from the August 3, 1861, *Harper's Weekly* shows the sisters being arrested by Union troops. They were accused of using their feminine wiles to lure Union captain Elisha Strong Kellogg to their home where he was captured by the Confederates. Apparently the sisters, ages 18 and 20, respectively, upon meeting the Union captain at his post implored him to walk them to their home beyond the Union line, as they feared going alone. Once there, Confederates, who had been waiting nearby, captured him. Several days earlier, two other Union soldiers had also disappeared near the Scott residence. After Captain Kellogg's capture, the two sisters stayed at a neighbor's house where they themselves were captured and, as the engraving shows, taken to General Tyler himself for questioning. They maintained their innocence and were released. The three captured Union soldiers turned up in Richmond, Virginia, as prisoners of war.

America Virginia Scott, the older of the infamous Scott sisters, is pictured in the 1890s. After the war, she married another secessionist, her cousin John Robert Darne, and lived in Falls Church until her death in 1926. She is buried in The Falls Church graveyard.

This photograph of a review of the 17th New York Infantry was taken near Minor's Hill in the vicinity of Falls Church c. 1861. The hills around Falls Church were used as federal fortifications for the defense of Washington. At various times during the war, it is likely that as many as 2,000 federal troops were posted within 2 miles of the village. (Courtesy Library of Congress, Prints and Photographs Division.)

An 1861 graduate of the University of Maryland, Falls Church resident Dr. Louis Edward Gott volunteered in the Confederate army and served as a surgeon. He was captured outside of Gettysburg and put into military prison for three months. After his release, he continued his military service until the end of the war. After the war, he returned to Falls Church where he remained for the rest of his life.

Clover Farm House, owned by Williston Clover and seen here in a modern photograph, was built c. 1851. In 1861, troops from Maine encamped around it. During the war, many farms and buildings in the village were damaged and/or looted by troops seeking food, wood, and valuables. It did not matter whether the property belonged to Southern or Northern sympathizers, all was fair game.

Col. John S. Mosby and His Confederate Raiders

Col. John S. Mosby (standing second from the left) led a band of partisan Confederate rangers in local raids against Union troops and supporters. On October 18, 1864, John B. Reed (or Read), pictured here, a Union man who had established a school for African Americans in his house after the Emancipation Proclamation became law and was also a member of the Home Guard, was captured and executed by Mosby's men. Frank Brooks, a black member of the Home Guard, was also killed, making it the bloodiest day of the war for Falls Church villagers. "That Baptist preacher Reed got what was coming to him," said one of Mosby's men. Mosby granted Reed's wife and daughter safe passage to what is today the Hunter's Mill area to retrieve the body. He is buried at The Falls Church graveyard.

The story of the William Henry Shreve family during the Civil War, especially his daughter Barbara Ann Shreve, reads like a novel. The Shreve's were devout Confederates, and both of William's children, son Benjamin Rutherford and daughter Barbara Ann, aided the Confederates and, in particular, Col. Mosby and his rangers. Barbara Ann acted as a spy for Mosby, and on one occasion, after obtaining "valuable papers," she was almost caught by Union troops. She made it to her family home, Mount Pleasant, and when the troops appeared, she was very calmly seated in the parlor. When the Union captain asked her to stand so she could be searched, she smartly replied that a Southern lady was never asked to stand for a gentleman. The captain apparently somewhat rattled by this, withdrew his request, and departed Mount Pleasant. Barbara Ann, of course, had been sitting on the papers and immediately dispatched them to Mosby. In this 1890s photograph, Barbara Ann, is pictured third from the right in front of Mount Pleasant. The house burned down in 1962.

This towering oak tree, which stood at the corner of W. Broad Street and N. Virginia Avenue, was known as Hangman's Tree. According to an unsubstantiated legend, Col. John Mosby ordered his men to hang Union soldiers from this tree in retaliation for similar treatment of his men. The tree was cut down in 1968 after suffering damage during construction, and a marker was put in its place.

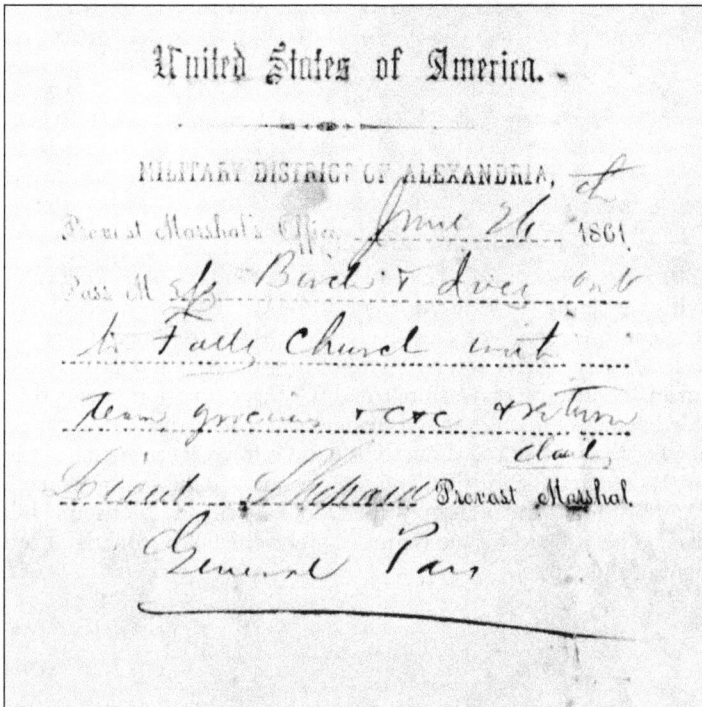

This military pass signed by the Union provost marshal allowed Falls Church residents Birch and Ives (probably Joseph Birch and George Ives) to travel across the Union line from Alexandria, Virginia, with a team of horses and groceries. One assumes that these two men traveled to Alexandria to purchase groceries and supplies for those villagers remaining in Falls Church.

Rutherford B. Hayes, prior to his becoming the 19th president of the United States, served as a Union major in the 23rd Ohio Volunteer Infantry and for several months was stationed at Upton's Hill. In his September 4, 1862, letter to his wife, Lucy, he described how the hills and forts around Falls Church were a key point in the defense of Washington, D.C. "Our situation now is this: Washington is surrounded for a distance of from seven to fifteen miles by defensive works, placed on all the commanding points. For the present the thing to be done is to keep the enemy out of the capital until our new army is prepared for the field and the old one is somewhat re-cruited. We . . . are placed to guard important roads and points of which Upton's Hill and Munson's Hill, Forts Ramsay, Buffalo, and 'Skedaddle,' all in the same vicinity, are the chief. We are about seven miles from Washington, in sight of the capitol."

Three

RECOVERY SPURS GROWTH
1866–1879

After the Civil War, the Falls Church–area secessionists who had endured the war and the Unionists who were returning from safer havens set about normalizing their lives and their relationships. Many properties were severely devastated and required considerable effort to reestablish. A new inflow of northerners seeking cheap land built new farms and stores. Civil War–era veterans, who had been stationed near Falls Church and found the area to their liking, returned, built homes, and made an impact on the community.

In December 1865, the 15th Constitutional amendment ratification finally ensured freedom for the slaves. Some blacks in the Falls Church area were already free. Several noted Unionists gave and/or sold land to blacks on the "Hill" south of the old Fairfax Road, and in the late 1860s, it became the site of a freedmen's village with a large number of black refugees. Here, in 1867, the black Methodists built a church/school (now known as Galloway) and the Second Baptist Church.

By 1870, Reconstruction was complete with black suffrage, restored statehood, a fourth state constitution, and a slowly recovering economy. The stress of war and subsequent Reconstruction led many to succumb to the demon rum; in 1867, the new lodge of the Independent Order of Good Templars held their temperance meetings in the Star Tavern. Others found renewed strength in religion, and the Episcopal, Presbyterian, and Baptist congregations were supplemented by four new churches erected by southern Methodists, Catholics, northern Methodists, and Congregationalists. With the assistance of federal government reparations, The Falls Church and Columbia Baptist Church were repaired and their congregations reorganized.

The town was incorporated in 1875 with about 500 people. The town council levied taxes, started the first public school (classes were held in the Baptist church), and extolled temperance. The Fairfax and Georgetown Turnpike (Lee Highway) was initiated, and the train was connected to Washington, D.C., allowing a new colony of government workers to commute from and to Falls Church.

Within just a few years, Falls Church would recover from the affects of war.

George Thomas (left) and Frederick Forrest Foote Sr., shown in a late-1860s tintype, were born into slavery and after emancipation went on to become well-respected members of the Falls Church community. Falls Church was more racially tolerant than many areas of Virginia. African Americans were part of the fabric of the community, having businesses and living peacefully side by side with their white neighbors. (Courtesy Henderson House Inc.)

Immediately after the Civil War, a number of churches were erected in Falls Church. The Galloway United Methodist Church, shown in a 20th century photograph, was built on Annandale Road in 1867 as the Methodist church for freedmen. A schoolhouse at the rear of the church housed the first organized African American Sunday school in Falls Church.

Fairfax Chapel's Methodist congregation, which split over secession, remained split after the war and organized into southern and northern congregations. The southern group met for a while in The Falls Church and then arranged to build Dulin United Methodist Church in 1869 at E. Broad Street on land donated by William Dulin.

This c. 1909 photograph shows the interior of the Dulin United Methodist Church. Of particular note are the hanging oil lamps. The actual building of the church was done by members of the congregation, assisted by two African American boys from Alexandria, who made the brick from local clay. The church was extensively remodeled in 1892 and again in 1927 when the entire building was pebble-dashed and stuccoed.

Maj. M. S. Hopkins, a Union officer, returned after the war to build this impressive home called Arringdon Hall, which was situated at 223 N. Washington Street. The style of the house, with its four stately columns, is what many might consider to be antebellum in style. It was demolished in the mid-1960s. (Courtesy University of Virginia, Special Collections Department.)

The freedmen Second Baptist Church was organized in 1870 by Rev. Hiram Read, a white minister and teacher who was the former pastor of the Columbia Baptist Church. The church held services in a two-room log cabin until this church was built. By the time of this photograph, this building had been abandoned in favor of a new church built in 1922 on Costner Drive.

The northern congregation of the Methodist church was the smaller of the two, having less than 20 members at the end of the war. They would meet at Isaac Crossman's house and also held services in the basement of the Columbia Baptist Church. In 1874, they raised funds for a church, and Isaac Crossman donated the land. The Crossman United Methodist Church on N. Washington Street was dedicated in August 1876.

Isaac Crossman was a highly respected citizen and a man of considerable wealth as his July 1900 obituary noted: "A large portion of the town of Falls Church is built upon land which he originally owned. Through his thrift and industry, he accumulated quite a respectable fortune."

Shown in the mid-1890s, the Colonial Revival–style Isaac Crossman house was built c. 1871. The house was originally located on N. Washington Street but in 1983 was moved to another Falls Church location to make room for commercial development—a fortunate happenstance, as many of the Falls Church Victorian houses have been torn down to make way for new development.

Highland View, a Second Empire–style home, was built in 1870 by Samuel Norment owner of the Washington and Norfolk Steamship Line. He looked all over Northern Virginia for the perfect spot for his summer home. Perched high on a hill in West Falls Church, this spectacular home was a little too isolated and lonely for his young and active daughters. In 1871, it was sold to Edmund Flagg.

This 1870 three-story, brick, Gothic Revival addition to the original clapboard farmhouse known as Mount Hope was erected by Capt. William A. Duncan, who purchased the 95-acre farm from Amzi Coe. The exterior look of this S. Oak Street house has changed little over the years.

This 1870 brick residence built in the Colonial Revival style was originally part of a 95-acre farm. From 1938 to 1943, Dr. Milton Eisenhower owned the home, and for a brief period his brother Gen. Dwight D. Eisenhower stayed here. Still standing today on E. Broad Street, Tallwood, as it is known, bears little resemblance to the house pictured.

Pictured is the original Saint James Catholic Chapel established on Fowler Street in 1873. Initially a mission of St. Mary's Roman Catholic Church in Alexandria, the priest from St. Mary's came once a month to celebrate Mass in the Sewell home, which stood on the hill west of St. James Cemetery. St. James became a separate parish in 1892. The church building was constructed on land donated by Sybilla Sewell and was built of wood and clapboard with clear-glass windows. After a new church was built on Park Avenue in 1902, this wooden chapel was torn down. The two stained-glass windows that had been above the altar were obtained by the Columbia Baptist Church. The St. James cemetery is still located at the Fowler Street site.

One of Falls Church's most prominent citizens was Judge Joseph S. Riley, owner of Cherry Hill Farm. He played a major role in the incorporation of the town in 1875; at his own expense, he traveled to Richmond, Virginia, and lobbied for the Act of Incorporation. In addition to being an alderman, he was a magistrate and justice of the peace and held court sessions at Cherry Hill.

Dr. John J. Moran served as the newly incorporated town's first mayor. He might be best known, however, as the attending physician to Edgar Allen Poe when Poe died in Baltimore in 1849. Dr. Moran wrote several pamphlets and would give lectures about Poe's final days. This photograph, taken sometime between 1868 and 1875, is the only picture of Dr. Moran.

Mary Speer Birch, pictured with her husband, Joseph, was a leader in the ladies' mid-1870s crusade against liquor sales in Falls Church. Specifically, she and other Falls Church ladies of high moral and spiritual character were against liquor being sold at John D. Brush's saloon located on Broad Street. Brush, a Confederate veteran, built the two-story saloon with a two-deck porch, and soon the porch, steps and all, became a gathering place for the male population. The saloon was a source of embarrassment to the community, and the ladies decided to do something about it. They maintained a vigil on the front steps of the saloon, singing hymns and reading appropriate scriptures. This led to an uncomfortable feeling amid the saloon's customers, and business soon fell off. The saloon closed much to the satisfaction of the community, and Falls Church remained "dry" for many years.

Charles E. Mankin bought the Brush saloon building, probably in 1881, and converted it into a store that initially sold toys, confections, and baked goods. He also sold the first yeast in Falls Church, which was made by his cook. Pictured in 1904, the store had expanded to include dry goods and notions. At Charles's death, his wife, Ann Valinda, took over the daily operations.

After much destruction during the Civil War, The Falls Church was repaired with the help of reparations paid by the federal government. From 1866 to 1873, church services were held there periodically after which, with the church repaired, the congregation reorganized, and the church reopened. In this photograph, it is possible to see the repairs to the bricks where the windows had been torn out.

Located at 137 N. Washington Street, George W. Hubbell built this clapboard house about 1875 on land purchased from the farm of Williston Clover. The house passed through several hands, and at some point, additions were made, including the half-octagonal tower. In 1979, it was sold to a local developer and subsequently demolished in 1981.

By the time Hollywood Farm was offered for sale in 1876, the farm was already over 120 years old, with the farmhouse having been built *c.* 1750. Note that the advertisement stresses the farm's proximity to the railroad, and that Falls Church is "where Intoxicating Liquors are not permitted to be sold, and where lawyers and doctors do not flourish."

Albert P. Eastman came to Falls Church during the Civil War and wanted to settle here, which he did in 1876. He built this home in East Falls Church about a year later. Eastman was very active in civic affairs, being a charter member of the Village Improvement Society. The house, including the white picket fence, is still there.

The Eastman's obviously loved birds. In the previous photograph of the Eastman home, two large birdhouses, including one that looks very much like the one being made here by Frank Eastman, can be seen to the right of the house. In 1903, the Virginia Statue Audubon Society was organized at Falls Church to "protect our native birds . . . and to promote a popular interest in bird study."

The Congregational Church, a Gothic-style building, was completed in 1879. The main audience room seated 300, with a Sunday school room in the rear. It has been used as a police station, town hall, library, meeting hall, and a general store. The building still stands on N. Washington Street, but the bell tower has been removed.

The Capt. L. O. Parker house (also known as the Keith house), built sometime during the 1870s, is a classic example of Second Empire style, featuring a mansard roof, brackets beneath the eaves, and dormer windows that project from the roof. During the Grant presidency (1869–1877), Second Empire was a popular style for government buildings, and home builders followed suit. This home was located at 221 Great Falls Street.

Falls Church was known for its beautiful trees, fruit orchards, and fine gardens. Most of those trees and plants came from Munson's Nursery, which was established in 1852 by Timothy Munson, a native New Yorker. His son, Daniel O. Munson inherited the 260-acre Munson Hill Nursery in 1869. Daniel, a Northern sympathizer during the Civil War, had the distinction of being kidnapped by Col. John Mosby and, to his good fortune, managing to escape. The Munson nursery business was very successful; his biographer called him "a mighty successful horticulturist." Daniel once wrote, "I am very busy, having from 20 to 30 men to attend in my nursery and also 40 agents to look after." Over the years Munson donated many trees to the town, including the silver maples that at one time lined Broad Street. The family home at Munson Hill was built in 1859.

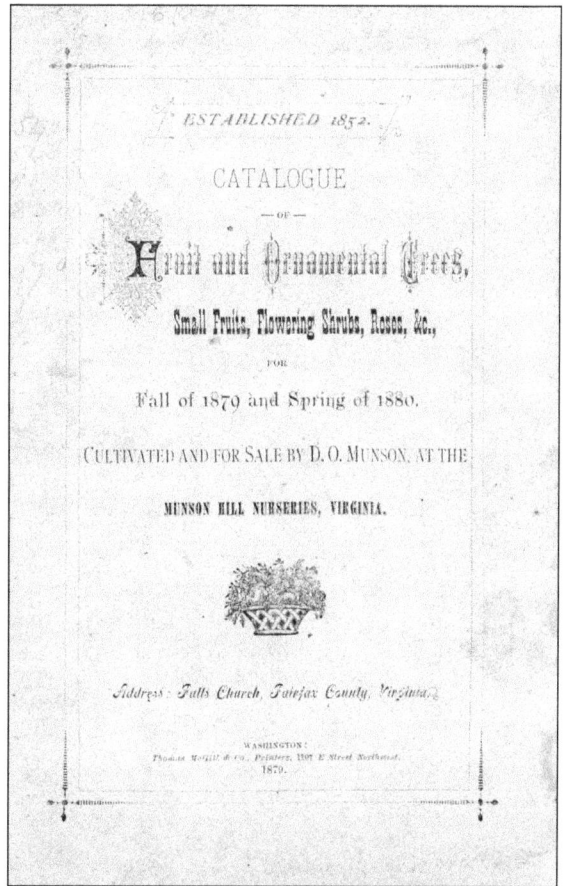

This 1878 map shows the town of Falls Church as having approximately 4 square miles with about 100 homes, 11 commercial structures, and 8 churches, a remarkable number for a town with the population of Falls Church.

Four

THE TOWN FLOURISHES
1880–1889

At the beginning of the 1880s, Falls Church had 677 inhabitants, including 263 blacks. Most residents were farmers, but more and more various types of workers, including those who commuted to federal offices and other jobs in Washington, were making Falls Church their home.

The decade was one of advancement and progress. The large, brick Jefferson Institute, paid for by private contributions, would be completed; concerned citizens formed a Village Improvement Society to preserve both the natural and man-made environment and to promote cultural activities; local businessmen started a telephone company; and a post office opened in the west end of town, giving Falls Church three post offices.

An 1890 map shows a new east-west southern boundary for the town south of the old Fairfax Road and the Leesburg and Alexandria Turnpike. The sizeable southern part of town, with 32 structures and a quarry, was gerrymandered in 1887 to Fairfax County by the Virginia General Assembly. The Democratic Party, who controlled Falls Church politics because more than 26 percent of the registered voters in this district were black and consistently voted Republican, requested this action. Most of the blacks lived in the gerrymandered part, but some others were residents elsewhere. All blacks were free; men could vote, more and more were educated and economically secure, some owned land, and a few, such as Frederick Foote Jr., were fully accepted into the predominantly white community. After gerrymandering, the town census counted a population of 792.

By the end of the decade, the town would have 134 structures, including 109 residences, 15 commercial structures, and 9 churches. The attractive small town of Falls Church had an emerging pattern of life characterized by community involvement and a certain charm and serenity.

Incorporated in 1875, Falls Church erected their town hall on the 100 block of S. Washington Street in 1880. It was a simple, frame building with a bell that was rung for council meetings and fire. By the time this photograph was taken, the building was used as the police station. It was torn down in 1953.

The Falls Church Presbyterians began meeting in the 1840s in the home of Amzi Coe, and by 1850, services were being held in Groot Hall. In 1884, they built this Gothic Revival church of stone from the local quarry. The red stone trim came from Seneca, Maryland, via the C&O canal. The church, which is still standing on E. Broad Street, has had additions made to it.

Looking quite dapper in this studio photograph, Frederick Forrest Foote Jr. was the first black man elected to the Falls Church Town Council, serving from 1881 to 1889. Prior to that, from 1876 to 1880, he had served as the town sergeant. A prosperous merchant, he owned a large grocery and provisions store at the corner of Broad and S. Washington Streets. Upon his death in 1889, the town council passed a resolution of honor, and members of the community served as pallbearers. (Foote election notice courtesy of Henderson House Inc.)

This is to certify, that at an election held in the Town of Falls Church, County of Fairfax, State of Virginia, on 27th May 1880, pursuant to the charter of incorporation approved March 30.1875. *Frederick F. Foote Jr.* was elected Councilman of said Town for the year beginning July 1, 1880.

In witness whereof, I hereunto place my hand and official seal this seventh day of June 1880.

Schuyler Duryee

Town Clerk.

The Jefferson Institute school building, located on the 200 block of Cherry Street, "was completed in 1882 after a period of some 6 or 7 years of organization and fund raising, during most of which time classes were conducted in the old Columbia Baptist Church on E. Broad Street. The money was raised by the people of the Falls Church community, by subscription. Fairfax County furnished the seats, blackboards, water buckets, and paid the teachers. The basement had two rooms—a school room in the front and a furnace room in the back. The first floor had two class rooms, and the top floor had a large stage across one end, and seats in the rest of the room. . . . Three teachers took care of all who came, and taught from the first to the eighth grade. Each teacher had from 40 to 60 pupils. . . . With our fathers, we children gave the school a lovely flag, a dictionary, a bible, and a clock for the Principal's office." That is how former student, Ada Walker, remembered the Jefferson Institute.

Isaac Crossman's daughter Susie Ann strikes a pensive pose in this *c.* 1885 photograph. The Crossman's were people of means, and it shows as Susie is dressed immaculately in a well-tailored bustle gown. Her photograph, like most of the other studio photographs in this book, would have been taken in Washington, D.C., or Alexandria, Virginia, since Falls Church did not have a photography studio.

The Village Improvement Society (VIS) of Falls Church was established in 1885 and is modeled after the Laurel Hill Association of Stockbridge, Massachusetts. Its objective was "to improve and ornament the streets of Falls Church by planting trees, cleaning and repairing sidewalks, and doing such other acts as shall tend to beautify and adorn the town." The brick sidewalk clearly evident in this *c.* 1900 postcard was a VIS project.

Throughout the 19th century, farming was important to the economic growth of the area as a burgeoning population in Washington increased the demand for more fresh foods. Isaac Crossman, as evidenced by this 1885 clipping from the *Virginia Register*, owned one of the best farms in the Falls Church area: "Next week we will give some description of another Falls Church farm, one of the best, belonging to Isaac Crossman. A new crib has just been built . . . to hold a portion of his big corn crop—estimated at 400 barrels. Yield of wheat of the farm this season is about 1,100 bushels!" These two photographs, from the early 1900s, were taken on the Crossman farm.

The Archibald Sherwood family home, pictured sometime in the 1880s, was built on the 217-acre farm that was originally owned by his wife's family (the Francis Fish family). In 1905, the Sisters of Perpetual Adoration from Louisiana established a school on this site and a convent to house the school's teachers. Today St. James School is located on the site.

Rev. B. W. Pond

Rev. Benjamin W. Pond, pastor of the Congregational Church, built this home located on Cherry Street in 1883. The house, as pictured here, is Victorian Gothic in style, but several alterations have been made to the house since it was first built, and the central facade has been altered as well.

57

Opened in 1883 by James W. Brown, Brown's Groceries and Hardware is a Falls Church institution. While the building and merchandise have changed over the years, it is still owned by the Brown family and is in business today (as Brown's Hardware). An 1885 advertisement stated "Dealer in Groceries, Provisions, Queensware [cream colored earthenware], Hardware, Paints, Oils, and Varnishes. Keeps constantly on hand a full stock of the above which he is selling low for cash."

In this photograph, taken sometime in the late 1880s, Mary Edwards Riley, Kathleen C. Mercer, and Jay H. Sypher, from left to right, stop and enjoy the view from Chain Bridge, which crosses the Potomac River into Washington. The girls, both corseted, wear bustle dresses, a style that would be out of fashion by 1890.

Almost hidden behind the trees, the Eagle House Hotel, pictured in 1904, was located on Park Place. A Falls Church landmark for many years, an 1885 advertisement boasts "It is located high, and cool, with pleasant surroundings for summer boarders. And in winter it is heated by steam; making it a pleasant and healthful place for people of the north who desire to spend their winters in a warmer climate."

Louisa Mars Henderson moved to Falls Church about 1900 and along with her husband, William, bought an acre of land next to The Falls Church. They built a home at 121 N. Washington Street and operated a grocery store in the community for many years. In this c. 1885 photograph, Louisa is pictured with two of her sons, Edwin Bancroft (standing) and William Alonzo. (Courtesy Henderson House Inc.)

This large, Stick-style home, built by William H. Nowlan, was completed in 1885. Because of the regular train service into the city, more government employees started moving from Washington, D.C., out to Falls Church. While the house is still standing, it has undergone considerable alterations over the years.

From left to right, the DePutron children—Lillian Corrine, Marian Beatrice, Edith Sophia, and Maurice Bentley—dutifully posed for their portrait c. 1888. Although the background looks to be outside, this portrait was actually taken in a studio in Alexandria, Virginia. Note the French bisque head doll that has been casually placed by the pedestal. (Courtesy Catherine Speakman.)

George Rollins, a Treasury Department employee, built this exceptional Queen Anne house in 1888. It has 20 rooms, 4 baths, 5 fireplaces, and a full basement. A unique feature is the large front tower, which is octagonal on the first floor and circular on the second floor. Located on E. Columbia Street, in this photograph the house had just been completed.

This 20th century photograph of the Rollins house front hallway gives some idea as to the beauty and quality of the home. The large entryway has wood paneled wainscoting and a tiled fireplace with wooden mantle and an iron fireplace insert. The steps lead up to a landing with windows of beveled and leaded glass. (Courtesy Library of Congress.)

Among powers given the town council by the new town charter was the authority "to provide and protect shade trees." In 1889, silver maples, shown some 20 years later, were donated by Dr. Nodine and local nurseryman D. O. Munson and planted along Broad Street. They were cut down in 1948–1949 when W. Broad Street was widened and in 1958 on E. Broad Street.

The Spofford and Church pharmacy, which opened sometime after 1886, was co-owned by Merton E. Church, a pharmacist who would become one of Falls Church's leading businessmen. The store had the town's first telephone exchange, a sign for which can be seen at the left. Based on the store's signage, it sold much more than just drugs. A large selection of oil lamps can be seen in the right window.

Guy Northrop Church is out for a ride in his wicker baby buggy, and he has stopped in front of his father's store to have this charming photograph taken. In the store window is a Diamond Dyes display. Diamond Dyes was a well-known brand of dyes that were used by thrifty housewives to recolor straw hats and refurbish old clothing.

In 1888, the Falls Church Telephone Company, founded by such town notables as Schuyler Duryee, Dr. T. M. Talbott, D. O. Munson, and M. E. Church, was incorporated and given the right to erect lines of wire and to connect with other lines. The poles for the telephone lines are clearly visible in this early-20th-century postcard of Washington Street, one of the main streets in town.

Joseph B. Tinner, pictured in an undated photograph, was the son of Charles and Mary Tinner. In 1890, freedmen Charles and Mary Tinner bought two and a half acres of land in Falls Church, built a house, and by subdividing to their children, they established what is now known as the Tinner Hill community. Both Charles and son Joseph were excellent stonemasons; the quarry where they cut pink granite was at the bottom of the hill that bears their name. Many of the Falls Church homes and buildings built during the Victorian era used this Falls Church granite. Joseph was recognized as a leader and powerful speaker, when he spoke people stopped and listened. In 1915, when the Falls Church Town Council voted to residentially segregate the town, Edwin B. Henderson encouraged Joseph to take the lead of the Colored Citizens Protective League, which in 1918 became a rural chapter of the NAACP. His strong voice and presence was instrumental in the assuring the civil rights of black citizens.

Five

TROLLEYS AND TROOPS
1890–1900

The 1890s were a time of continued growth and development in Falls Church. The Village Improvement Society (VIS) is credited with improving the character and culture of the village in many ways. They built brick sidewalks with oil lamps and in 1891 planted the trees along Broad Street. Because of the town meetings and cultural events VIS held, such as the Independence Day activities, everybody knew everybody.

While the nation suffered from a financial depression in the early 1890s, Falls Church progressed well. During the decade, Falls Church continued the evolution from farm community and cool summer retreat for Washington to a permanent home location for many people, mostly government employees. Falls Church made history when it offered the first modern subdivision in Virginia. New, beautiful, Victorian homes began to fill in the community, many on smaller parcels. In 1897, an electric trolley line into Washington was a convenience that made Falls Church a very attractive location to many.

Even though the professional class emerged and was gaining status, the culture still held a high place for landholders. Falls Church had many gentleman landowners. Orchards and farms flourished throughout the area as avocations of those in the professional ranks working in Washington. The village was bustling with activity.

New technologies began to emerge. Telephone poles and lines became a normal part of Falls Church landscape. For the first time, the most fashionable homes in Falls Church were built without fireplaces or mantles because they had central heat.

The end of the decade brought Falls Church an influx of activity. From May to September 1898, Falls Church bustled with soldiers and visitors from the large, newly established Camp Alger, a 1,400-acre troop training facility located west of town during the Spanish-American War. And in 1899, Mattie Gundry opened her progressive school for mentally handicapped children, the only one in the South at the time.

As one century came to an end, Falls Church was positioned to embrace the new one.

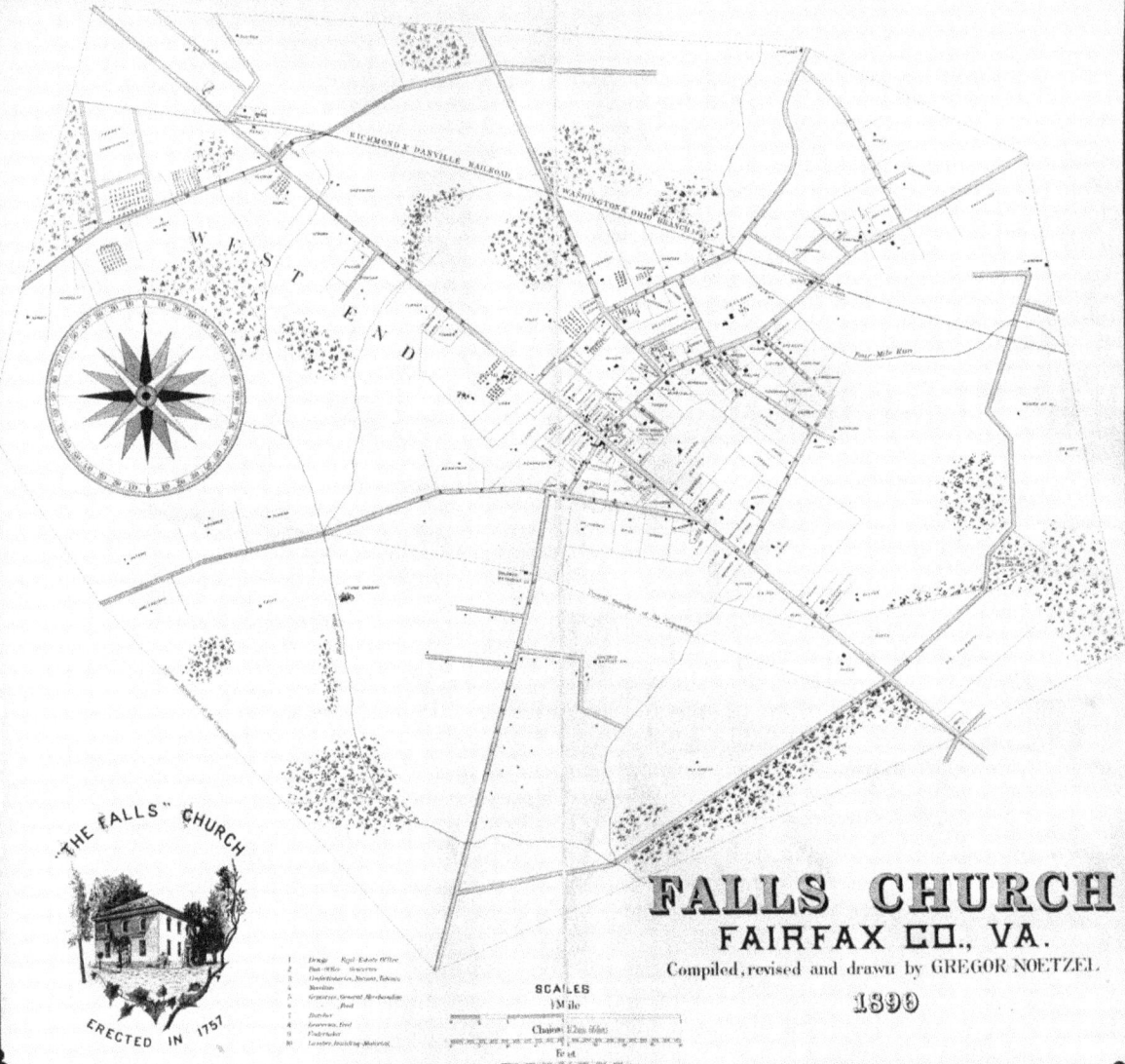

By 1890, Falls Church had clearly established itself as a town with a downtown business area surrounded by homes and farms. The turnpike (Route 7) was now identified as Broad Street, the main street running east and west through town.

This fanciful Queen Anne Victorian, built in 1890, was located at 271 N. Washington Street. An architecturally interesting house, it featured shingle and clapboard siding, sawn-wood trim, and an asymmetrical plan that was unusual in Falls Church. It's most distinguishing feature, however, were the bull's-eye windows in the cupola. This photograph shows the former Victorian beauty as it nears demolition in 1971.

In this c. 1890 photograph, William Nathan Lynch and his family (twins Will and Cora, wife Sarah, and baby Talbot) pose in front of their house, which was located in the 100 block of E. Fairfax Street. Lynch owned a feed store and blacksmith shop, which was located behind his residence. The man holding the horse is one of Lynch's blacksmiths. The home has been demolished.

The Independent Order of Odd Fellows, Falls Church Lodge No. 11, was organized in October 1890. Shortly afterward, largely through the generosity of Charles E. Mankin who gave both the land and money for the project, this brick building was erected at 248 W. Broad Street. The *Evening Star* newspaper called it a "monument" to the memory of Charles Mankin. It was demolished in 1970.

Located on Fulton Avenue, this 1890 Queen Anne, gabled house with the impressive wraparound porch is known as "Woodland." The 25-acre property was originally part of Cherry Hill Farm, and the Cyrus Birge family lived there from 1898 until the 1920s when the tract was split up into smaller lots.

Woodbrook, an 1890 Queen Anne–style house located on Fowler Street, was built by J. Owens Berry. For indoor plumbing, there was a cistern in the attic that was supplied water pumped by the windmill. The windmill, which was installed at the time the house was built and is the only windmill still standing in Falls Church, was used until the 1930s.

Mary Elizabeth Sherwood DePutron was the only child of Archibald and Lucinda Fish Sherwood, one of the oldest families in Falls Church. She inherited the Sherwood family property, which in 1891 was broken up into parcels and sold through the Falls Church Improvement Company. This would become the appropriately named "Sherwood" subdivision, one of the first housing subdivisions in Virginia. (Courtesy Catherine Speakman.)

In June 1891, a special train from Washington brought 400 people to the Sherwood subdivision, and 92 lots were sold in one day at the aggregate price of $23,000. Even though it was Mary Sherwood DePutron who had inherited the 217-acre Sherwood farm, it was her husband, Jacob DePutron, who was listed on this advertisement. In the Victorian era, the sale of real estate was considered the domain of men.

This photograph, *c.* 1891, celebrates Edith Sophia DePutron's graduation from St. Mary's Seminary, a girls' secondary school in Alexandria. She was valedictorian of her class. At that time, public education in Virginia was mandated only through seventh grade, so parents that wanted to further their children's education had to send them to private schools or to public school in Washington, D.C. (Courtesy Catherine Speakman.)

The First Ladies Aid Society "in Dr. Rathbun's pastorate" (Presbyterian church) gathers on the porch at Auchmoody Place *c.* 1891. Ladies Aid Societies had their start during the Civil War and continued into the 20th century. They usually worked on charitable causes but sometimes supported social reform such as the temperance and the women's suffrage movements.

Dr. Birdsey Northrop, pictured, was a national proponent of Arbor Day. After a powerful storm destroyed many local trees, Dr. Northrop visited Falls Church and proposed to the Village Improvement Society that it inaugurate an Arbor Day to include schoolchildren to replant the school yard. "Arbor Day was celebrated on Monday last [April 25] . . . After the exercises in the hall the ceremony of tree planting took place and one hundred trees were planted on the school house grounds, and the rest in different sections of the town," reported the *Fairfax Herald* on the first Arbor Day celebration in Falls Church and the state of Virginia. After the ceremony, the children posed on the school steps for their photograph. Each April, Falls Church continues the tradition with the planting of trees and a public celebration at the original site.

James Isaac Brown was a much beloved principal and teacher at the Jefferson Institute grammar school, serving from 1890 until his early death in 1893. Many years later, former student William H. Ellison remembered Brown's "remarkable ability to teach persons at different ages with such skill that they forgot neither the subject taught nor the teacher . . . the best teacher we ever had."

Jacob and Mary DePutron built this two-story, gabled Queen Anne–style house on Lincoln Avenue about 1893. Mary would not have a fireplace in the house as she recalled from her childhood the unpleasant task of polishing the brass fireplace fenders. The property has been preserved.

Pictured is the interior of the Falls Church Bakery, located on Broad Street, with its proprietor, George Erwin, pictured second from the right. The bakery advertised homemade bread, pies, and cakes and that bread and orders were delivered daily without extra cost.

Built about 1893 by George Erwin, the house located on Great Falls Street, is an example of a Queen Anne–style house with Stick-style influences. It features shingles, clapboard, panels, and two projecting balconies. A small barn at the rear is where the delivery horses for the Falls Church Bakery were housed.

In 1894, George T. Mankin, Jesse Parker, Maydie Watkins, and Margaret Birch are ready for a ride in the "surrey with the fringe on top." The Falls Church livery stable was run by E. J. Northrop, the proprietor of Eagle House, so perhaps the friends rented the surrey for their outing.

The blacksmith was a necessary and important part of every Victorian community. For many years, the Lynch family operated the blacksmith shop on E. Fairfax Street near The Falls Church. In 1906, Robert Harmon, shown in a 20th-century photograph, bought the business and operated it until he retired in October 1957.

In 1894, George Albertson and his wife, Charlotte, built this lovely Stick-style home on Little Falls Street. The family called it "The Triangle" since the property it was situated on was triangular. The home is still standing today.

The Boernstein house, with its impressive witches cap turret, is a striking example of late Victorian-era architecture. Large houses such as this, however, were expensive to maintain and often fell into disrepair, which led to many of them being demolished. This house, located on Little Falls Street, was torn down in the 1970s to make way for the Falls Church recreation center.

The Dr. Tunis C. Quick house stood opposite the Boernstein house at the corner of Little Falls and Great Falls Streets. The sign at the front door, which at that time was on Great Falls Street, bears Dr. Quick's name. This house was demolished in 1978 for a townhouse development.

Dr. Tunis C. Quick and his new bride, Virginia Thorne, pose for their April 21, 1897, wedding photograph. Her dress style, with its leg-of-mutton sleeves, was very popular in the mid-1890s. Dr. Quick was well known in the community and at one time served as the head of the Falls Church Board of Health.

On September 2, 1895, Charles A. Stewart and his family enjoyed a round of croquet on the front lawn of their East Falls Church house. Note that Stewart is dressed in a suit and tie; in the Victorian era, "casual" clothing did not exist. Stewart would never have considered being outside without having a tie, jacket, and hat on.

George A. L. Merrifield, an 1874 arrival from Maine, was another of those who worked for the federal government and made the hour-long commute into Washington by train. He built this large and imposing Queen Anne–style house of clapboard and shingles with Eastlake-style trim on N. Washington Street. It was completed in 1895 and originally had 10 rooms and 2 baths. Fortunately, this structure has been preserved.

Seated on a rustic bench in his conservatory, Albert Eastman enjoys a leisurely read in this 1895 photograph. Conservatories first started appearing in houses during the Victorian era when the advent of indoor heating systems made it possible to maintain a variety of houseplants. The Victorians loved plants and nature and whenever possible brought it into their homes. With their collection of plants, the Eastman's were no exception.

Ready to attend the lawn at the Albert Eastman home in East Falls Church, this is the Victorian version of a riding lawn mower or roller. Most of the Falls Church residences had a fair amount of land around them and successful men such as Albert Eastman could hire help to take care of the lawn and grounds.

John Wells, funeral director and embalmer, stands in front of his small-looking funeral parlor at East Falls Church. His parlor likely contained coffins and various other items necessary for a proper Victorian funeral. In those days, the dearly departed was normally laid out at home, most likely in a family member's parlor, for viewing by family and friends.

Large, extended families were the norm during the Victorian era, with grandparents, parents, children, stepchildren, aunts, uncles, and cousins often living in the same general location. The Isaac Crossman family, shown in a reunion photograph, is no exception. Isaac is pictured standing sixth from the right.

Even in small towns there were exclusive clubs and it would appear that the San Souci (French for "without care") club was the one in Falls Church. An invitation to one of the San Souci dances made clear that the invitation was "positively not transferable, and must be presented at door." A dance card such as this one would have been presented to both male and female attendees upon arriving at the dance. Prior to the music beginning, the gentlemen would have asked the ladies for a particular dance and it would be noted on the dance card so that both would remember who they were to dance with. Strict rules of etiquette dictated how the gentleman was to ask for a dance and the number of times a lady could dance with the same gentlemen.

"A large crowd has been gathered around from the town and vicinity around the building all day and great indignation is expressed but apparently no great effort is being made here to find the guilty parties" is how the *Evening Star* newspaper reported the 1896 burglary attempt at Brown's store. Two unidentified men used dynamite to blow open the safe, which also blew out the front of the store.

Dr. Thomas M. Talbott, pictured with his wife and son in 1897, settled in Falls Church in 1871, becoming the first doctor in town. Although he considered himself to be an old-fashioned horse-and-buggy doctor, he was also progressive. In 1888, he caused a stir by introducing the telephone to Falls Church with a single-line hookup between his house and the village store 2 miles away.

Home House was built in 1897 by Charles E. Mankin for his wife, Ann Valinda, on property given by his mother-in-law. When built, it was considered modern and was open for several weeks for public inspection. Home House was originally painted "Virginia Mode" (light gray) with dark gray trim and green shutters and roof. The home, now demolished, was located in the 200 block of W. Broad Street.

Mankin's Pharmacy, established in 1898 by George W. Mankin, was located on N. Washington Street, right in the heart of the business district. Maude Nowlan Edmonds, a longtime Falls Church resident, remembered the convenience of stores located on Broad and Washington Streets when one could call a store, place an order, and have it delivered right to the front door.

An electric trolley line reached East Falls Church in 1897, and by 1901, the trolley tracks extended along Lincoln Avenue to West Falls Church, parallel to the steam railroad. Combined with the railroad, it offered transportation to Leesburg, Alexandria, Fairfax, Washington, and many intermediate points, thus becoming a major factor in the growth of the town. The tracks were used until 1939 when trolley service ended.

In January 1898, the battleship *Maine* was sent to Havana, Cuba, to protect United States' interests during a time of civil disturbances. On the evening of February 15, a terrible explosion rapidly sent the *Maine* to the bottom of Havana Harbor, killing over 250 of the men on board. Falls Church resident, Charles Parker Galpin, was one of the fortunate survivors. "Remember the Maine" became the battle cry for the Spanish-American War.

The transportation system and available land were important factors in the choice of a 1,400-acre farm just outside of Falls Church for Camp Russell A. Alger during the Spanish-American War. Once Congress declared war on Spain on April 21, 1898, troops began pouring into Falls Church from May to September. As seen in this photograph, train and trolley service was vital to the throngs of incoming soldiers and their families. The horse-drawn carriages did a thriving business carrying soldiers and visitors to the camp. The large building in the middle is J. C. Elliott's store, and the building behind the trolley is Harry Moreland's blacksmith shop and stables. As Charles Stewart wrote, "The summer of 1898 was a most eventful one in Falls Church. No such stirring scenes had been witnessed here since the days of the Civil War. Troop trains arriving or departing, drills at camp and practice marches through the town, martial music from many bands, reveille and taps, all contributed to impress the town folk with the fact that the country was at war."

These tents set up at East Falls Church served as a receiving area for recruits. At the height of the troop buildup in August 1898, Camp Alger had 33,755 soldiers stationed there and 1,347 officers. Among these, 10 were from the Falls Church area. Falls Church resident Arthur I. Flagg died from typhoid fever while at the camp.

The majority of Spanish-American War volunteers were leaving home for the first time. For them, it was a time of excitement, a chance to travel and to visit places well beyond their family farms and small towns. A studio photograph, such as the one pictured, would provide the soldier's family with a fond remembrance of their patriotic sacrifice. (Courtesy Linda Lau.)

Writer Carl Sandburg (not pictured) who was stationed at Camp Alger but never saw battle wrote, "I lived in a tent, answered roll call six and seven times a day, cut saplings and built myself a bunk, more than once made a practice march in hot weather carrying the first weeks a . . . rifle, cartridge belt, canteen, and blanket roll." Such was the life of a soldier stationed at Camp Alger.

Although welcomed by the community, Camp Alger did cause problems for the locals. The increase in population caused severe shortages of drinking water, and the army had to bring in barrels of water. To keep order, provost guards were established at East Falls Church and residents disliked being stopped by army camp guards while going about their daily business. Temperance leaders also disliked the boomtown atmosphere around the camp.

On May 22, 1898, President McKinley and his wife, cabinet members, and foreign dignitaries arrived at Camp Alger for a Grand Review. With 15,000 troops on display, the review was designed to show the strength of the U.S. forces. As indicated in this 1899 engraving from *Harper's Pictorial History of the War with Spain*, the Grand Review was a proud moment for all. (Courtesy Linda Lau.)

In this 1898 photograph, George L. Erwin delivers mail to Camp Alger. In those days, Falls Church had three post offices—one in the center of town, the east post office, and the west post office. In the days of horse and buggies, physical distance made three post offices a necessity.

The Falls Church postal employees pose on the steps of the Broad Street post office in this summertime photograph c. 1898. Notice that the windows are wide open with no screens in them to help keep out flies and other insects. The lady is dressed in summer-appropriate attire, which includes her stylish "boater," a hat style that was popular for both men and women.

James Whitcomb Riley, a favorite poet of the era and a nephew of Judge Joseph Riley, would visit the judge's home, Cherry Hill, when in the area. Riley would sometimes give readings at Cherry Hill and also wrote a poem, "Out to Old Aunt Mary's," that is thought to be a tribute to the judge's wife and James's aunt Mary.

Merton Church and his wife, Clara, enjoy a cold ride down snowy Washington Street in a horse-drawn sleigh. Even in winter the roads had to be maintained by packing down the snow. During the 1880s and 1890s, Robert Nourse was responsible for maintaining the Falls Church roads.

Even with its close proximity to Washington, D.C., and the trainloads of people who came to the area during the Spanish-American War, Falls Church was basically still a small, rural town where many farmed and kept livestock. Maurice DePutron probably did not have to go far from home to find this friendly cow.

The Victorian era was one of fervent patriotism. This photograph, *c.* 1897, shows some smartly dressed friends gathered to hear an Independence Day speech on the lawn of the Eagle House Hotel. Sen. John W. Daniel of Lynchburg is said to be the speaker.

In an era when the average life expectancy was approximately 50 years of age, reaching a golden anniversary was a remarkable achievement. Jacques V. Quick and his wife, Sarah, were married in November 1848 and are shown celebrating their golden wedding anniversary with their 10 children. It is also quite remarkable that all 10 of their children lived to adulthood.

This house, which was located at 419 W. Broad Street, was the home of Henry and Georgia Taylor's family. Georgia was a maid, one of the few jobs available to black women during the Victorian era. Henry did gardening and carpentry work. As proper Victorians would be, they are dressed in their Sunday best for this photograph. The house has been demolished.

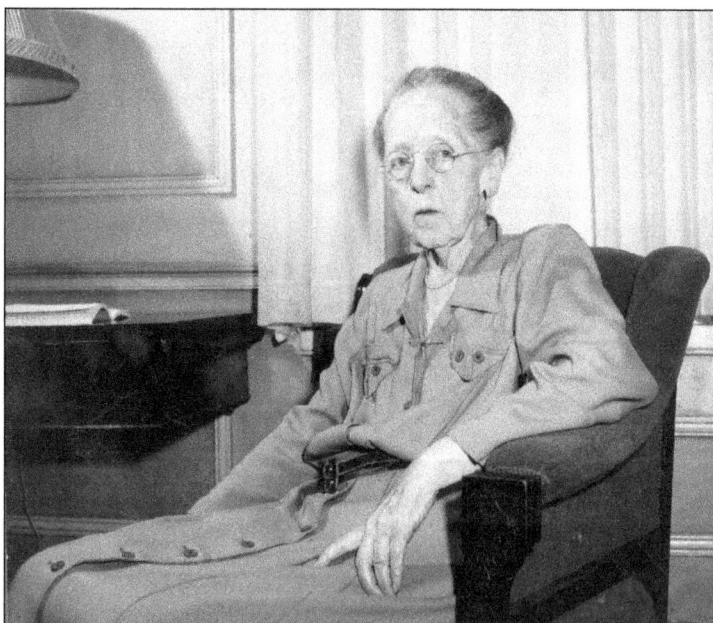

Mattie Gundry was definitely a woman ahead of her time. A college graduate at a time when most women did not get a college education, in 1899, she established the Virginian Home and Training School for mentally deficient children, and she served as its director for 50 years. After women got the vote in 1920, she was elected to the Falls Church Town Council where she served three terms.

Recognizing the need for a school in the South for the mentally deficient, Mattie Gundry searched for and found the Schuyler-Duryee house at 309 W. Broad Street. A large, substantial house, there were 33 rooms in the home and the three cottages. The school's brochure notes that "The great objective in this establishment is to give to children of affliction home comforts and care as well as thorough training in such exercises as are best suited to each individual case and to make them not only useful and happy but saved from a life of dependence and anxiety to parents." The children lived at the school with constant supervision by specially trained teachers. In addition to their studies, the students received training in music and art and, took part in religious services. This was a novel approach because in the Victorian era many with mental handicaps where relegated to a life in an asylum. The school was the only one of its kind in the South and later was considered the second largest in the nation.

As the Virginia Training School's brochure indicates, "the house is surrounded by beautiful and large grounds which afford ample room for play and exercise." This group of Falls Church friends, who are not students of the school, decided to take advantage of the lovely grounds and have a picnic. In 1948, the entire school was demolished to make way for a massive development of apartments.

From 1899 to 1906, the Falls Church library was located in a garage behind the Columbia Street home of George W. Hawxhurst. The Village Improvement Society had helped to amass a collection of books for circulation. The library's 1903 catalog boasted "a total of 650 books now in the library. New and popular books are constantly being added." The library was open three hours on Tuesday, Thursday, and Saturday.

Religion played an important part in the Falls Church community, bringing together family and friends every Sunday. This photograph of the Congregational Church Sunday school class on July 14, 1899, was taken on the steps of the Albert Eastman home in East Falls Church.

Lewis Crump is dressed like Little Lord Fauntleroy, a fashion style popular for boys in the 1890s. Born in 1892, Lewis died in October 1900 of diphtheria, an all too common disease at the beginning of the 20th century. Although Falls Church had a low mortality rate, epidemics of diseases such as diphtheria still occurred.

This c. 1900 photograph shows the East Falls Church railway station and Elliott's store, which also served as the trolley line ticket office. "During the Spanish American War tickets were 25 cents a round trip to Aqueduct Bridge. Then you had to walk across Aqueduct Bridge and take another street car in Georgetown," reminisced Goldie Elliott. The area changed dramatically in the 1960s with the construction of Interstate 66.

Dr. Louis Gott's wonderfully designed, Queen Anne–style residence, with its distinctive porch and fretwork, was located on Washington Boulevard in East Falls Church. Dr. Gott, a lifelong Falls Church resident and longtime doctor, "never lost a pneumonia case" according to one Falls Church resident. In 1936, Dr. Gott's residence and the rest of the area known as East Falls Church was ceded by court order to Arlington County.

Built in 1880 by William McElfresh Ellison and pictured at the beginning of the century, this store sold coal and wood, essential commodities for heating and cooking. The store had a small rope-operated elevator in it for moving supplies up and down. Located at the corner of W. Broad and West Streets near the Ellison family home, the building was torn down in 1955.

The DePutron children and their friends enjoy a leisurely summer afternoon get-together in the family's backyard. Even though outside, they would still be expected to maintain a certain decorum in their behavior and dress. (Courtesy Catherine Speakman.)

Located on E. Broad Street, the William Nathan Lynch family home was built c. 1898 in the Eastlake style. Son Talbot (on the horse) and the twins, Will and Cora, pose proudly in front of their home, which was only a couple of years old at the time of this photograph. Lynch, a prominent citizen, operated a feed store and blacksmith shop. The house has been preserved.

The Lynch family parlor, c. 1900, has all the trappings of a proper Victorian setting. A large oak mantle adorned with bric-a-brac, heavily patterned wallpaper, and wall-to-wall carpeting, an upright piano, lace curtains, a glass-domed cross, and a portiere door curtain give the impression of a prosperous and stylish family. Their son Talbot is looking at a stereopticon, the Victorian version of a Viewmaster.

The inscription on the back of this photograph says "the heart of East Falls Church at the turn of the century." To the left of the road is the Crossman farm with corn growing in the field. In the middle to the right of the road is the East Falls Church train station. All of these structures are long gone and the road is now Lee Highway.

The Falls Church women kept up on all the latest fashion styles. Only a train ride from Washington, D.C., they had their choice of a number of department stores and milliners. A day spent shopping and perhaps having tea in one of the department store tearooms would not have been unusual. The two stylish ladies in this c. 1900 photograph are Maude Riley (left) and Ada Walker.

Like many of the properties in Falls Church during the Victorian era, Arringdon Hall had much acreage and a large garden, including the vine-covered gazebo. One can only imagine how colorful and fragrant the garden must have been. (Courtesy University of Virginia, Special Collections Department.)

Brown's general store recovered nicely from the 1896 blast that blew out the front of the store, and the business continues to this day. In this undated photograph, Horace E. Brown, in the hat, is seated on the top front step. Notice the broom display in the background.

Six

An Era Ends
1901–1915

At the start of the new century, Falls Church was the largest town in Fairfax County, with 1,007 residents. A 1904 map of the town shows 125 homes and 38 properties from two to 132 acres in size that could still support farms and orchards. The town had become a center of commerce and culture, with 55 stores and offices and seven churches.

Regular train and trolley service into Washington, Alexandria, and Fairfax enabled townsfolk to work, shop, and attend schools in those places. It also encouraged visitors to the area; some called it "a summer resort for Washingtonians." Horse-drawn vehicles were still the preferred mode of transportation around town, but cars were starting to make an appearance. The need for an improved system of paved roads was becoming apparent.

The dynamic Mattie Gundry was the first woman to serve on the new Falls Church bank's board of directors. Literary and social groups encouraged recreational study and discussion of community improvement issues. New in town was a chapter of the Daughters of the American Revolution, the Falls Church Poultry Association, Civic League, and the Boy Scouts of America.

Like many small towns, Falls Church was experiencing some growing pains. Litter, vandalism, nonworking street lamps, and train noise were a few of the issues facing the town council. In 1912, Falls Church received electric service, thus eliminating the need for acetylene gas and oil lamps.

In 1915, a special census in Falls Church counted 1,212 whites and 166 African Americans (12 percent), and the town council defined a small residentially segregated district for colored as was permitted under a 1912 state law. This was contested by the newly formed Colored Citizens Protective League (which later became the first rural chapter of the NAACP), which successfully delayed the issue until it became moot by an unrelated U.S. Supreme Court decision.

Even though the Victorian era had come to an end, Falls Church maintained its Victorian look and feel longer than many communities; it did not go easily into the modern era.

Along with electric trolley service, railway train service to Washington, D.C., continued to have a major impact on Falls Church. Not only did the service allow more people to move to the area and commute daily into Washington, but it also made it possible for people to easily visit the area. As Charles Stewart wrote in 1904, "The Falls Church Inn [Eagle House], where an old Virginia welcome awaits the way-farer, accommodates transient and regular boarders. Besides there is the 'Evergreens,' a large summer boarding place which has a high reputation. There are numerous other homes, in or near the village, where boarders are taken for the summer months." As the Washington-Virginia Railway Company advertisement indicates, service was available all day and well into the night, enabling townsfolk and visitors easy access to Washington's stores, theaters, museums, and restaurants.

Elizabeth Morgan Styles, age six, and Francis Holmes Styles, age four, pose for a 1900 Easter photograph. The grandchildren of Judge Joseph and Mary Riley, they would spend their summers at Cherry Hill Farmhouse until they moved permanently to Falls Church in 1908. Elizabeth and Francis donated the land where the Falls Church Mary Riley Styles Public Library is now located.

J. C. Elliott's store was located in East Falls Church at Lee Highway and N. Fairfax Drive. As seen in the photograph, it was right between the electric trolley service on Fairfax Drive and the Washington and Old Dominion train tracks on the south. Elliott's daughter Goldie remembered, "Father had a delivery team of beautiful matched dappled grey horses. They were his pride and joy."

Taken from a 1901 postcard, this street scene shows the 100 block of Broad Street. The building with the porch is Star Tavern. The small building to the left is George Thomas's shoe shop. George, a former slave who came to Falls Church after the Civil War, made boots and shoes for several generations of Falls Church citizens and was a highly respected citizen of the community.

This August 1902 photograph is of the Loving Cottage on Maple Avenue. The three Thurber brothers—William, Robert, and James (who would become the famous writer)—are on the porch along with their mother and a neighbor. James remembered when his father was employed in Washington that "my mother couldn't stand the heat of the city and so we rented this house on Maple Avenue."

"Our garbage was collected by an ancient white-haired negro, not more than five feet tall, whose two-wheeled oxcart was pulled by a brace of oxen. His appearance never failed to enchant us boys, for he was not only out of the South, but out of the past, even out of fiction," is how James Thurber remembered Falls Church's first garbage collector, "Uncle" Pete Gillham.

With a growing congregation of about 325 members, the St. James Catholic parish built a larger and more conveniently located church on Park Avenue in 1902. Built of native sandstone from the local quarry, A Virginia Village claimed the church was "one of the finest specimens of Gothic architecture in Northern Virginia." In 1952, it was remodeled and enlarged.

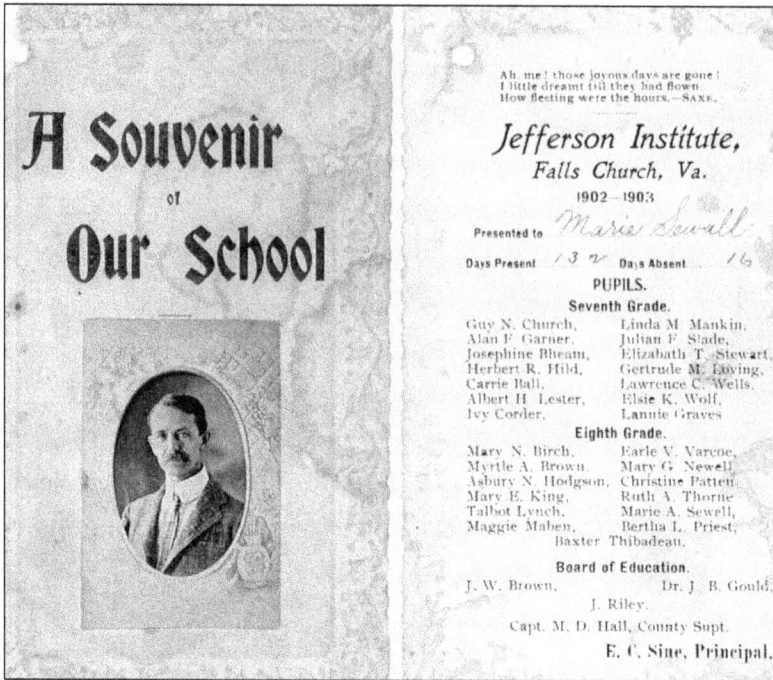

A Souvenir

of

Our School

Jefferson Institute,

Falls Church, Va.

1902–1903

Presented to *Marie Sewall*

Days Present *132* Days Absent *16*

PUPILS.

Seventh Grade.

Guy N. Church,	Linda M. Mankin,
Alan F. Garner,	Julian F. Slade,
Josephine Rheam,	Elizabath T. Stewart,
Herbert R. Hild,	Gertrude M. Loving,
Carrie Ball,	Lawrence C. Wells,
Albert H. Lester,	Elsie K. Wolf,
Ivy Corder,	Lannie Graves

Eighth Grade.

Mary N. Birch,	Earle V. Varcoe,
Myrtle A. Brown,	Mary G. Newell,
Asbury N. Hodgson,	Christine Patten,
Mary E. King,	Ruth A. Thorne
Talbot Lynch,	Marie A. Sewall,
Maggie Mahen,	Bertha L. Priest,
	Baxter Thibadeau.

Board of Education.

J. W. Brown,   Dr. J. B. Gould,

J. Riley,

Capt. M. D. Hall, County Supt.

E. C. Sine, Principal,

The Jefferson Institute students listed in a 1902–1903 souvenir had reached a milestone in their education. It was the end of the school year, and as the poem at the top of the program states, "those joyous days are gone!" Some students would head off to high school, others might find jobs. For young women like Marie Sewall, the choices would be limited.

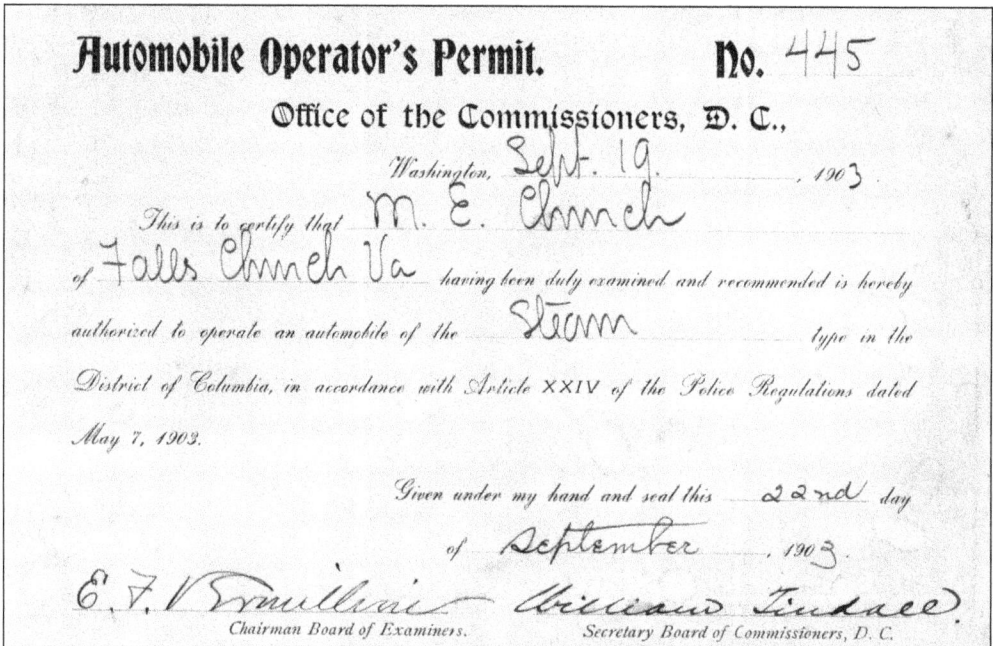

Automobile Operator's Permit.   No. 445

Office of the Commissioners, D. C.,

Washington, Sept. 19 . 1903 .

This is to certify that M. E. Church

of Falls Church Va *having been duly examined and recommended is hereby*

authorized to operate an automobile of the Steam *type in the*

District of Columbia, in accordance with Article XXIV of the Police Regulations dated

May 7, 1903.

Given under my hand and seal this 22nd *day*

of September . 1903 .

E. F. Vermillion   William Tindall

Chairman Board of Examiners.   *Secretary Board of Commissioners, D. C.*

Merton Church, a progressive, must have been one of the first Falls Church citizens to have a driver's license and to own that new-fangled invention, the horseless carriage (in this case steam powered). Automobiles were expensive novelties in the early 1900s, and only the well-to-do could afford them and the maintenance. Is it any wonder that Church was a strong proponent of better roads?

M. E. Church

REAL ESTATE, LOANS AND INSURANCE

TWENTY YEARS' EXPERIENCE

Suburban Property and Investments in Fairfax and Alexandria Counties Given Special Attention

Attractive homes, beautiful villa sites and good building lots in Falls Church, Livingston Heights, Ballston, Clarendon and all the Alexandria and Fairfax suburbs for sale on Easy Terms.

Money Safely Invested in First Trust on Real Estate

Consult Me Before Investing

WRITE FOR INFORMATION   TELEPHONE CONNECTIONS

M. E. CHURCH, FALLS CHURCH, VA.

Maybe Charles Stewart put it best when he wrote, "In the development of Falls Church, Mr. Church has been indefatigable, and has been personally identified with every progressive movement." With unusually high business acumen, Merton E. Church managed to be at the forefront of a wide variety of progressive business ventures for over 50 years. Starting out as a pharmacist and store owner, he branched out into real estate and insurance, organizing the Falls Church Improvement Company, of which he was general manager. He was a cofounder of the Falls Church Telephone Company and a founder of the Falls Church Bank. He also built the first electric light system in Arlington and Fairfax Counties and was responsible for saving the Northern Virginia to Washington railway service from extinction. Church also served on the Falls Church Town Council and as mayor and was involved in many other civic and church-related organizations. In the late Victorian era, no one in the community was more involved or important than Merton E. Church.

Even in her pince-nez glasses, Eva Birch, in this 1905 photograph, is the epitome of the Gibson Girl. Created by illustrator Charles Dana Gibson in the 1890s, the Gibson Girl was considered the personification of the feminine ideal—an hourglass figure, expertly upswept hair, and a poised, independent air about her. Eva's beautiful dress features a pouter pigeon-style bodice so called because it puffs out in the front.

"A bank is needed," lamented Charles Stewart in his 1904 *A Virginia Village*. At that time, Falls Church residents had to travel to Washington, Alexandria, Fairfax, or Leesburg to do their banking. In 1906, Falls Church got their bank, which opened on July 30. The wooden bank building would eventually be replaced by a more impressive bank constructed of native granite from the local quarry.

The John William Garner family has gathered in front of their Columbia Street home to celebrate July 4, 1906. On the porch are Robert, Katharine, Lily Freeman, John William, Betty, and Alan Freeman. The two ladies standing by the tree are unidentified.

Taken from an early postcard, this image shows Broad Street, the main street running east and west through the town, long before automobiles would take over the street. Notice that Broad Street is a dirt road. Carroll Shreve, whose plumbing business in the early days used horses and wagons, remembered that "The roads were terrible. When it rained Broad Street was a quagmire."

In 1907, Edith Sophia DePutron and Wilbur Alexander Speakman were married and had their wedding photograph taken in the left front parlor of the DePutron family home. Edith, pictured second from the left, is outfitted in a beautifully designed and hand-detailed dress that remains in the family to this day. (Courtesy Catherine Speakman.)

Family legend has it that Edith DePutron Speakman was an excellent horsewoman. She is riding her horse "Nellie" sidesaddle, which in the Victorian era would have been the way a lady would have been taught to ride. Not only was it considered improper for a woman to straddle a horse, but the long dresses made it nearly impossible to do so. The DePutron home is in the background.

In 1907, Minnie Ellison, wearing a beautiful white, summer dress, stands next to the water well behind the family home on W. Broad Street. At the time, Falls Church families still had to rely on wells and cisterns for their water and indoor plumbing needs. Falls Church would not have a town water supply until 1936.

The Rust House on N. West Street was built sometime between 1907 and 1910 in the Shingle style. A distinguishing feature of the house is the three-story water tower that was used to feed water into the house. The water tower has now been converted into guest quarters. The one-story building to the left is a combination acetylene gas and ice house.

Most families kept livestock—horses, cows, pigs, chickens, etc.—in the yards of their houses. In this photograph, dated 1909, Carroll Shreve is milking the family cow in the backyard of his house on W. Broad Street. In 1910, the town council renewed an ordinance that made it unlawful for "any cow, ox, horse, mule or hogs or other animals to graze on any of the sidewalks or highways."

Having the school photographer show up was just as important then as it is today, documenting significant milestones in a child's life. This photograph taken in 1909 is of the fourth-grade class at the Jefferson Institute. Elizabeth Tabb Stewart, teacher of the fourth-grade class, is pictured third from the left at the top.

112

During the early 1900s, the Columbia Baptist Church had a substantial increase in its membership. It was during this time that a lot on the corner of Washington and Columbia Streets was purchased with the idea of building a new, larger church of stone. The first service was held in the new church on the fourth Sunday of June 1909. The stained-glass windows over the pulpit are the windows from over the altar of the original St. James Catholic Church. The original 1909 Columbia Baptist Church is still intact, but it has had significant additions made to it.

Summerfield Taylor's market, shown *c.* 1910, was located at E. Broad and Washington Streets right in the heart of town. Gas-powered streetlamps, like the one in the foreground, were installed in 1893. On May 25, 1893, the *Evening Star* newspaper reported that the Falls Church "street lamps are all up and were lighted for the first time last night."

In this undated photograph, these two men seem pleased to stop and have their picture taken, even in the snow. This picture was taken on E. Columbia Street near the Crossman Methodist Church. Both men are carrying books, perhaps on their way to a church service. Both men also wear bowler or derby hats, a popular style from the 1850s up to the 1920s.

In 1894, Congress passed a law recognizing the first Monday in September as Labor Day, an official national holiday. Like many communities, Falls Church used the opportunity not only to recognize the contributions of the working classes but also as an end to summer. In this 1909 real photo postcard, the citizens of Falls Church are enjoying a Labor Day athletic competition.

Falls Church did not have a lot of heavy industry, but they did have a steam-powered gristmill. The Rosslyn Milling Company, located on what is now N. Oak Street near the railroad tracks, ground corn, wheat, and feed for the farmers in the area. This photograph is from 1910; in 1912, lightning struck the building, and it burned to the ground.

In the days before radio and television, companies had to go directly to the cities and towns to market their products. In 1909, the Quaker Oats company introduced its Puffed Wheat and Puffed Rice ready-to-eat cereals. This cleverly designed automobile, with a "puffer" on top, was one means of getting the attention of the Falls Church residents.

The unnamed gentleman in the photograph is obviously a satisfied customer of Brown's general store. The general stores in towns such as Falls Church would have to provide a wide range of merchandise in order to meet the needs of its customers. One resident reported that Brown's was the most "general" of general stores, selling everything from groceries to hardware.

Photographs of Victorian interiors were often made to commemorate a particular occasion such as a wedding or party. In these photographs, the Birch family is celebrating an event, but it is not clear what the event is. There are streamers of hearts hanging in every room that might lead one to think of Valentine's Day, a wedding shower, or perhaps even the wedding. The photographs were obviously staged, as certain items have been carefully placed in each of the rooms and the photographs were taken by a professional photographer making one believe that the Birch family considered this an important occasion in their lives. Photographs such as these give a good idea as to what the interior of a typical Victorian house looked like at the time.

Mother Birch caringly attends to her daughter in a bedroom that is furnished with an oak bedroom set. The daughter, getting ready for her "event," sits in front of a large dressing table whose mirror allows a perfectly sized reflection for this interesting and well-thought-out photograph.

The ladies gathered in front of the Birch family home for this 1910 photograph are, from left to right, (first row) Dode Coddington, Minnie Ellison, and Elizabeth Brunner; (second row) Helen Martin, Marguerite Fennell, and Mary Birch. The Jefferson Institute, located at 203 Cherry Street, can be seen in the background. The stately brick building was demolished in 1958.

Dr. Edwin B. Henderson and his wife, Mary Ellen, were noted educators and civil rights activists. In 1904, Edwin became the first black American in the country to be certified as a physical training instructor. He was also a writer in the field of athletics, authoring *The Negro in Sports*, and was a major figure in establishing equal rights and opportunities for black athletes. Mary Ellen, principal at the Falls Church Negro School, fought for and was eventually successful in obtaining equal resources for black students. Leaders in the African American community, they were determined activists, fighting against segregated residential districts in Falls Church and segregated sports facilities in the Washington, D.C., area. In 1915, they were instrumental in organizing the Colored Citizens Protective League, which later became the first rural chapter of the NAACP. (Courtesy Henderson House Inc.)

The maintenance of roads was a top priority whether one had a horse and buggy or an automobile, as either was prone to getting stuck in the mud. As seen in this Fairfax County photograph c. 1911, early motorists often needed help on the unpaved roads. In was not until after World War I that the roads in and around Falls Church would be expanded and paved.

On July 21, 1912, the last day of the Peace Jubilee commemorating the 50th anniversary of the Battle of Manassas, Pres. William Howard Taft left Washington, D.C., via automobile (he was the first president to have a car) for Manassas, Virginia. On the way, he stopped by the home of his friend Dr. Tunis Quick for dinner and to deliver a speech from the Quick's front porch.

This home, which was located at 200 Pennsylvania Avenue, was built in 1898 by Block and Berney, developers from Washington. It was the first home of the Sylvester Parrott family, who are shown c. 1910. In 1912, Hy Anderson bought the house for $1,200. Anderson's son James remembered "We ran a small dairy. . . . People used to come and buy chickens, vegetables, eggs, and milk. . . . The most we ever had at 200 Pennsylvania was 10 cows. It was all hand milking. I did a lot of it. To make the deliveries, father would roust us out at 5 in the morning. . . . He and I would head for the barn. Mother would start the fire in the old wood stove, and while that got going, she would go out and feed the chickens. When she got through she made us breakfast. We would bring the 'milk' to the dairy in our basement. We strained and bottled the milk, and put it in water to cool with the caps off. After breakfast we put the caps on." The house was demolished in 1962.

When this interesting office photograph was taken on February 14, 1912, the business world was definitely the domain of men. Only one woman, a Miss Christenson, is visible in the photograph; she was probably a stenographer or typist, office jobs considered suitable for a woman in the early 1900s.

LOVE   SACRIFICE   SERVICE

The Lincoln-Lee Legion

ABSTINENCE DEPARTMENT OF THE ANTI-SALOON LEAGUE
I HEREBY ENROLL WITH THE LINCOLN-LEE LEGION AND PROMISE WITH GOD'S HELP
TO KEEP THE FOLLOWING PLEDGE

WHEREAS, THE USE OF INTOXICATING LIQUORS AS A BEVERAGE IS PRODUCTIVE OF PAUPERISM, DEGRADATION AND CRIME, AND BELIEVING IT IS OUR DUTY TO DISCOURAGE THAT WHICH PRODUCES MORE EVIL THAN GOOD, WE THEREFORE PLEDGE OURSELVES TO ABSTAIN FROM THE USE OF INTOXICATING LIQUORS AS A BEVERAGE.

A SOBER NATION AND A SAFE HIGHWAY

NAME_____   DATE_____

THE DUPLICATE OF THIS PLEDGE IS DEPOSITED AT THE NATIONAL OFFICES OF THE LINCOLN-LEE LEGION, WESTERVILLE, OHIO

COPYRIGHT 1903, BY HOWARD H RUSSELL   COPYRIGHT 1903, BY THE ANTI-SALOON LEAGUE OF AMERICA

Falls Church had a long history of supporting temperance causes. The Falls Church Independent Order of Good Templars (IOGT), organized in April 1867, had as its purpose the prohibition of liquor traffic by the will of the people. This early-1900s Anti-Saloon League pledge card was found in the papers of one of Falls Church's most prominent citizens. The Anti-Saloon League and the IOGT worked together to dry up Virginia.

Shadow Lawn on Little Falls Street was built sometime before 1878. At the time this photograph was taken c. 1912, it was the home of the Dr. Roue L. Hogan family. In 1920, Mattie Gundry bought the property for $10,000 and turned it into a sanitarium named Whitehall. The house is still standing today but bears little resemblance to the original home.

Written on the back of this photograph that was taken at Shadow Lawn in 1912 is "Uncle Abe with Betty." Uncle Abe, one of the Hogan's servants, may have lived in the servant's quarters, located in a separate building at the back of the driveway. Horses were still the preferred means of local travel, but it would not be long before the automobile would overtake them in popularity.

Dr. Hogan's daughter Enid and William Smyser enjoy a Shadow Lawn hayride on a cart pulled by Dolly. Scenes such as this would have been common place in Falls Church, where many families had enough land to have small farms, orchards, and livestock.

Dr. Edwin B. and Mary Ellen Henderson built this charming Colonial Revival bungalow in 1914 and lived there until 1965. The house remains in the family to this day. (Courtesy Henderson House Inc.)

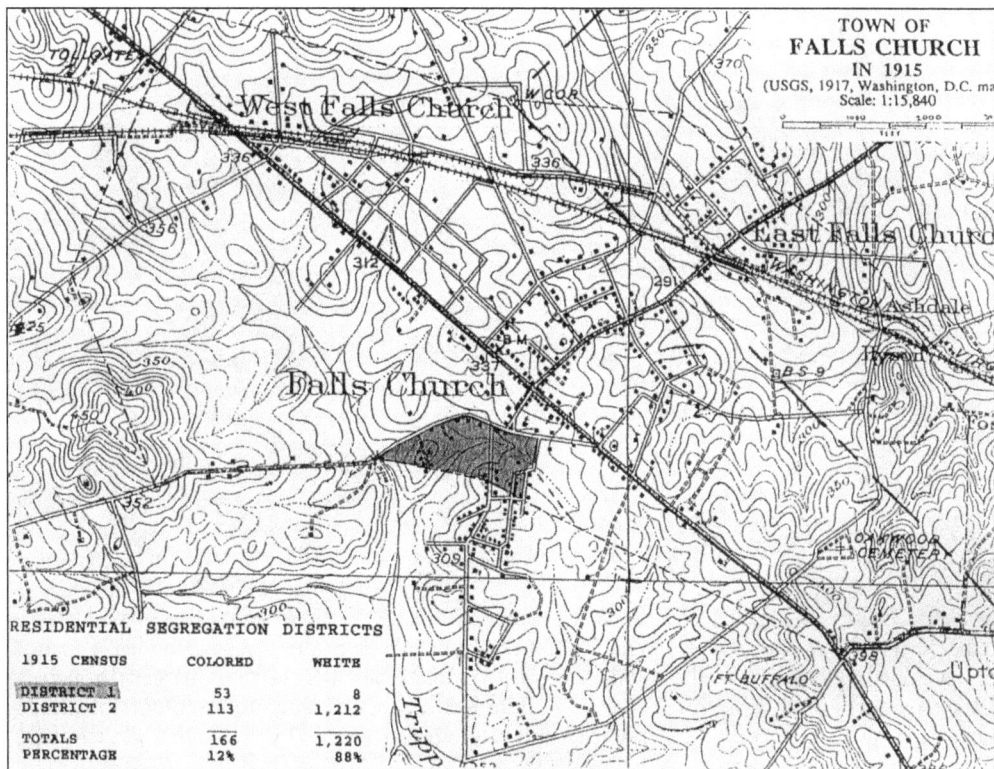

RESIDENTIAL SEGREGATION DISTRICTS

1915 CENSUS	COLORED	WHITE
DISTRICT 1	53	8
DISTRICT 2	113	1,212
TOTALS	166	1,220
PERCENTAGE	12%	88%

In response to a 1912 Virginia law, the Falls Church town council adopted an ordinance that created residential segregation districts in the town. The shaded area of this 1915 map shows district one, the area established by the town council as a "colored" residential district. For those blacks living in district two, they did not have to move out but could only sell to whites. The ordinance was never enforced.

Dr. Thomas M. Talbott was one of the first Falls Church residents to own an automobile, which enabled him to get to his patients faster. However, a 1916 town law made it illegal for automobiles or horses to go faster than 12 miles per hour.

This 20th-century photograph of the 300 block of Little Falls Street gives some idea as to how undeveloped it was right in the middle of town. "From Little Falls you couldn't get through on Park [Avenue] to [Washington Street]. . . . The Keith property encompassed part of what is now Park Avenue. They had blackberries and raspberries there and you couldn't get through," remembered James Anderson.

Well into the 20th century, farms such as this one continued to be part of the Falls Church landscape. There were several dairy farms in the area and, as late as the 1940s, Roberts poultry farm operated on West Street within the town limits. In its appearance and spirit, Falls Church remained a Victorian community for a half century more. (Courtesy Henderson House Inc.)

BIBLIOGRAPHY

Camp, Shirley. *Past Times Around Falls Church: The Change from Plantation to Village and Town 1729–1875*. Baltimore: Gateway Press, 1997.

Douglas, H. H. *Falls Church: Places and People, Volume I.* Falls Church, VA: The Falls Church Historical Commission, 1981.

Falls Church Village Preservation and Improvement Society. *Falls Church: Historical News and Notes.* Falls Church, VA: The Falls Church Village Preservation and Improvement Society, 1993.

Gernand, Bradley E. *A Village Goes to War: Falls Church During the Civil War.* Virginia Beach: The Donning Company Publishers, 2002.

———— and Nan Netherton. *Falls Church: A Virginia Village Revisited.* Virginia Beach: The Donning Company Publishers, 2000.

Harrison, Noel Garraux. *City of Canvas: Camp Russell A. Alger and The Spanish-American War.* Falls Church, VA: Falls Church Historical Commission, 1988.

Steadman, Melvin L. *Falls Church: By Fence and Fireside.* Annandale, VA: The Turnpike Press, 1964.

Stewart, Charles A. *Falls Church (A Virginia Village).* Falls Church, VA: J. H. Newell, 1904.

Stuntz, Connie Pendleton, *A View of Falls Church, Virginia, thru the 1881–1889 Diaries of Edmund Flagg, Esq.* Falls Church, VA: Higher Education Publications, Inc., 2005

Wrenn, Tony. *Falls Church: History of a Virginia Village.* Falls Church, VA: Historical Commission of the City of Falls Church, 1972.

———. *Cherry Hill Farm.* Falls Church, VA: Historical Commission of the City of Falls Church, 1971. Revised, 1977.

Visit us at
arcadiapublishing.com

www.ingramcontent.com/pod-product-compliance
Lightning Source LLC
Chambersburg PA
CBHW050606110426
42813CB00008B/2476